Architectur
and landscape

RIITTA
NIKULA

Architecture and landscape

THE BUILDING OF FINLAND

OTAVA PUBLISHING
COMPANY LTD
HELSINKI

Graphic design and layout:
Markku Reunanen and Sinikka Lindfors

Translation: Timothy Binham

Paper: Kymex Cote Matta 130 g/m^2
Kymi Paper Mills Ltd

Otava Printing Works
Keuruu 1993

ISBN 951-1-12534-6

Contents

A. Ahlström paper mill in Varkaus.
Erkki Kairamo 1977.

Preface

This book is intended to serve as a first general introduction to its subject. My imaginary reader is the tourist who wonders why Finland looks as it does today.

I shall start with an outline of the Finnish landscape, the setting for its buildings. I shall examine architecture primarily as a history of building, disregarding unbuilt plans, even those which hold an important position in the history of ideas in Finnish architecture. This is not a chronicle of dreams or heroes but mainly the story of how Finland was built.

The predetermined brevity of the book made the choice of sites extremely difficult. In seeking a fair balance, to my regret I had to omit numerous significant trends, especially from our own century. This is a pity considering that Finland's building stock is among the world's youngest – almost 90 per cent of it was built after 1920. Modern architecture is also an important ingredient of Finland's international image. My only consolation is that a number of books specializing in the 20th century have already been published.

My main facts on older architecture are gleaned from the *Ars Suomen taide* (The Art of Finland) series, a joint effort by the entire corps of Finnish art historians. I therefore extend my general thanks to all my colleagues and hope I have not misunderstood them too badly. I particularly thank my friend Marja Terttu Knapas, who once again generously shared her invaluable expertise on old Finnish architecture.

Tapiola, June 1993
Riitta Nikula

SOTKAMO. Vuokatti Naapurin vaaralta.
N:o 456. Daniberg, H:fors.

Vuokatti hills, Sotkamo, at the turn of the century. Photo: I. K. Inha.

The foundation

I. K. Inha

Time and place

Finland, a large and still sparsely populated country, is located in the extreme periphery of Europe. Of its 340,000 square kilometres, almost 70 per cent is forested and unbuilt; some 10 per cent is covered by water. Finland is the seventh largest country in Europe, but with its five million people, it is only twenty-fourth in terms of population. The average population density is less than 17 per square kilometre.

In much of the country, buildings provide but a thin veneer over the solid natural landscape. Rapidly changing modern architecture coexists with the monumental inertia of geological time.

And yet Finland is part of Europe: its architecture is rooted in the Mediterranean tradition. Innovations have travelled north along different routes at different times. The meeting of East and West on Finnish soil lends our architectural history its special fascination. Adapted to barren conditions and scarce materials, the great styles have flourished here, reduced to the essentials of hard stone and solid wood.

By 1990, one quarter of the population was living in the southern province of Uusimaa, the only region in which population density exceeded 100 per square kilometre (124.8 in 1989). The now most populous area, however, was not settled until the first millennium A.D. An ageless island landscape frames the historic architectural strata of the early capital, Turku, as well as of Helsinki, developed as the capital during a century of Russian rule.

Finland extends from the 60th to the 70th parallel. Almost one quarter of its territory lies north of the Arctic Circle. Only the treeless fells of Lapland rise above the Northern conifer belt. Compared to the rest of Europe, Finland is a low country: its average altitude is only 152 metres above sea level.

Water and trees dominate the landscape. Almost three quarters of Finland's surface is covered by forest. A third major element is wetlands, which cover nearly one third of the country; in places, forest and wetlands overlap.

Finland emerged from its ice cover only 9,000 years ago. The receding ice masses moulded the basic features of the landscape, polishing the rock and creating the Finnish lakeland by making deep furrows which run northwest to southeast. Moraine ridges, or eskers, on top of the bedrock, following or facing the direction of retreat, fill in the details of how the ice withdrew and the climate warmed.

The earliest archaeological finds show that parts of southwestern Finland were already settled almost 10,000 years ago. As the ice retreated, Stone Age man followed in search of game. The first Finns hunted elk, beaver, seal, aurochs, and bear. Fishing was also important.

The signs of Stone Age settlement are few: all that remains are traces of primitive hearths. The dwellings of the hunters seem to have been small, light, conical *kota* huts, suggested by rows of concave depressions in the ground. Waterways were the main transport routes. The earliest settlements were on the coast or near lakeshores, on dry, sandy slopes running gently southward or westward, in places now far from water because of geological uplift which began after the Ice Age and still continues on the coast of the Gulf of Bothnia.

During the Bronze Age (c. 1500–500 B.C.), settlements became permanent along coasts and at the mouth of rivers. A belt of closely spaced tumuli follows the coasts of the Gulfs of Bothnia and Finland, testifying to the existence of a settled agrarian population. Permanent settlement was possible once food was available in the same place all year round. Building techniques developed; but little is known about the dwellings of the period. Artefacts are scarce, as all wooden materials have disintegrated. Finds of packed clay tell us that the Bronze Age people built square dwellings of upright poles supporting horizontal withes bound together to form walls.

The most imposing Bronze Age monuments in coastal southern and western Finland are tumuli known as *hiidenkiuas* (devil's stove), graves topped with an enormous pile of the biggest stones that could be carried. The largest

*Bronze Age tumulus,
Parainen.*

such barrows have a diameter of tens of metres. Not for nothing does Pekka Sarvas call them Finland's oldest public monuments. We know more about the ceremonies of prehistoric man than of his everyday life: the graves only contained the very finest objects, as the dead were fitted out as if they were going to a celebration. What we do know about everyday life and utensils has been deduced from much humbler finds.

The Iron Age began in Finland around 500 B.C. and ended with the beginning of recorded history on the west coast of Finland in the early 12th century, deep inland not until what in the rest of Europe were the late Middle Ages and after, during the 16th century.

The earliest agricultural settlements of the Iron Age were in southwestern Finland, spreading east to the provinces of Häme and Savo. Other pockets of population were in Karelia (Karjala) and southern Ostrobothnia (Pohjanmaa).

The great migrations (c. 400–650 A.D.) did not seriously affect the quiet course of events in Finland. As before, objects found show influences from the eastern Baltic and Germanic world. However, at the end of the period of migrations, a new era began – according to the archaeologists, the first distinctly Finnish culture. By this time, there were villages in the oldest settled areas, although most of the population lived in isolated dwellings even in the heartland.

The middle Iron Age was a time of progress in agriculture. Farming was by the slash-and-burn method, practised on the lands surrounding the houses with a rotation period of some 20–30 years. Progress was also made in animal husbandry. Finds show that the tools used for tillage also improved significantly. Iron ploughshares were attached to wooden frames; sickles and scythes were now larger.

Some of the finest relics of the Iron Age in Finland are primitive forts built atop steep cliffs. They were not permanent dwellings, but provided safety against aggressors. The natural protection afforded by the site was strengthened with earthworks and stone bulwarks, and with log structures. The large fort of Rapola in Sääksmäki in the province of Häme was built on a ridge. Inside the walls was an area some 380 x 200 metres square, which could be closed off with gates. The dwellings discovered along the Rapola ramparts are thought to have been night shelters for the castle guards.

The primitive forts were built mainly along the coasts of Varsinais-Suomi (southwestern Finland), on the north shore of Lake Ladoga, and in the lakeland of southern Häme. They have not been studied in sufficient detail to pinpoint the time of construction or the uses to which the buildings were put. Most of the forts were located along waterways, but roads are thought to have existed by the Viking period (c. 800–1050).

Granite furrowed by the ice sheet, Ikaalinen.

According to Pirkko-Liisa Lehtosalo-Hilander, Finland had developed a distinct culture of its own by the Viking era. No major military alliances were formed within its area, but some communities selected chieftains and organized concerted fishing, hunting, and trading expeditions. Some fortifications were built during the Merovingian period between the migrations and the Vikings (c. 600–800). Although Finland had neither kings nor towns, it did have ablebodied men and trading places when the Vikings began their raids to the east, sailing along the Finnish coast.

In the early 13th century, when Swedish rule and Christianity were gradually asserting themselves in Finland, the main settlements were still in the Åland Islands and the western provinces of Satakunta, Varsinais-Suomi and Häme. From the 11th century on, the growing influence of Novgorod brought eastern features to the culture of the Karelians on the shores of Lake Ladoga. For many centuries, Uusimaa remained a wilderness, a hunting ground for Finns and for Estonians from the south coast of the Gulf of Finland. The once flourishing southern Ostrobothnia languished during the Viking period.

Scholars have deduced the population of prehistoric Finland from the data of the earliest census in the 16th century, which suggest that the population around the year 400 was between 6,000 and 10,000. By the end of the prehistoric period, it was between 50,000 and 85,000. Thus, archaeologists are unlikely to discover any large community of builders from this period.

Stone

The Finnish landscape is simple and austere. Only three per cent of the surface is bare rock, but nowhere is the bedrock far from the surface. The bedrock consists of hard intrusive rock – granite, diorite and gabro – and of gneiss and various forms of schist. It forms part of the Fennoscandian bedrock shield. There are no soft, easy-to-work types of rock.

Sturdy grey granite dominates our image of mediaeval Finnish architecture. The wooden architecture of the time has disappeared, as has that of the prehistoric period. Five castles and several castle ruins remain, along with seventy-five churches and fifteen stone sacristies added to wooden churches, and a handful of fortified manorhouses. Our knowledge of mediaeval Finnish art is based on meagre evidence: only a total of some one hundred buildings remain, even counting those located in territory ceded to Russia after World War II.

A simplified variant of Gothic was developed in Finland, partly to replace the first wooden churches and imitating their forms. The rectangular main church halls were erected of enormous boulders of grey granite; the whole congregation took part in the construction. From the 14th century on, fine vaults laid of red brick were built over the granite walls, usually dividing the interior into three aisles. The ornamental gables of the high, Gothic-type roofs were built of the same red brick, in regional variants of the delicate forms of international Gothic. Fine moulded bricks for the window and door frames added a graceful note to the monolithic churches.

Lars Pettersson has provided a striking description of the aesthetics of materials in Finnish Gothic. "When in the Mediterranean countries the walls were built of brick, the openings were often framed with natural stone. Here, the church tended to be built of stone and the brick was saved for gables and openings. This might facetiously be called the 'turncoat principle'."

Wood

Finland was located in the coniferous forest belt even before the Ice Age, some three million years ago. After the ice melted, the climate became warmer: from 8,000 to 2,500 years ago, mixed deciduous and coniferous forests, hardwood species, and hazelnut trees grew far north of the present narrow southern belt. This was followed by a cooler period, during which pine

and spruce regained space. The spruce is the youngest tree in Finland: it spread in from the east, reaching the southwest coast of the country only 3,000 years ago.

Wood has always been by far the most commonly used building material in Finland: over 80 per cent of the current building stock is wood.

The horizontal blockwork technique, or corner-timbering, was adopted from the Russo-Byzantine civilization, probably during the ninth century A.D. This was virtually the only method of construction in rural areas up to the 1930s, and even in the 1950s one could still find local builders in country villages who could build a holiday home or a sauna by the traditional method of jointing pine logs at the corners. Not until then did industrialization take over in wood building, as the entire building industry underwent a radical transformation.

Every decision made when building with logs was based on solid logic. The master builder, with skills passed down from generation to generation, was fully aware of the limitations and potential of his material. The tools were simple, the most important one being the axe with which the tree was felled and the log carved to the form required for jointing. The lower side of the wall log was carved to a concave shape and fitted to the curved upper surface of the log below. This technique provided insulation. A two-pronged iron tool was used for fitting the

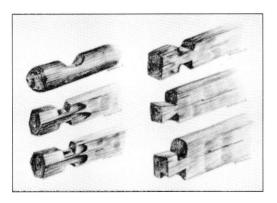

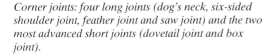

Corner joints: four long joints (dog's neck, six-sided shoulder joint, feather joint and saw joint) and the two most advanced short joints (dovetail joint and box joint).

The simple art of corner-timbering. Niemelä croft, Seurasaari island museum.

timber in place. A plumb line was used to ensure that the wall was straight; in large buildings, holes were drilled into the logs for wooden dowels which improved the stability of the walls.

A variety of joint forms adapted to different purposes were developed. In the more modest outbuildings, the simple, long crossing joint (or 'dog's neck') was used until the present century. With increasing wealth and carpentry skills, and as a result of increased western influence, the clients for important city buildings and, particularly, for churches, wanted walls as smooth as those of stone buildings. The walls were hewn and the corners kept at a level with the wall with a short locked joint. The dovetail joint and box joint were elegant, technically advanced solutions.

The saw was a latecomer in Finland: it was not needed in timber jointing. An axe-hewn log end withstands the weather better than a sawn log. With the rise of the sawmill industry, weath-

In the pine forest.

erboarding began to be used for churches and homes from the 18th century on. At the heart of the long building tradition was an expertise based on a profound familiarity with the properties of wood. The various features of western and eastern European architectural styles gradually made their way into corner-timbered houses over the centuries.

The only traces of the first corner-timbered buildings found in excavations are clay linings with a triangular cross section. These were long strips of clay pressed into the gaps between logs. When the buildings burned down, the clay hardened and was preserved over the centuries. Such linings were necessary at a time when jointing techniques were still primitive. One of the special qualities of wood is that the material disintegrates entirely over time. When the building is no longer needed, the wood disappears without a trace into the natural cycle through decay, rot, or fire. The logs of a building that had become too small or old-fashioned could be recycled, replacing the decayed lowest courses if necessary. Timber structures could also be moved from one place to another.

Pine was the best building wood. In past centuries, the tallest pine trees were felled for churches, the next best used for houses. Lower-quality timber was good enough for cattle shelters. Spruce was used occasionally, though it bends more easily and decays faster than pine.

Farmhouse harmony, Ruovesi local history museum.

Vernacular architecture

The landscape

The Finnish rural landscape readily reveals its prehistory, the era when the land was formed, to the perceptive traveller.

The agricultural landscape has passed through so many transitions since the wars that the best way to find the atmosphere of the vernacular tradition today is to visit an open-air museum. Old rural buildings have been preserved best in the remotest hinterland. Houses built before the nineteenth century are rare everywhere: the only large group of 19th-century buildings consists of the finest manors and farmhouses of the era. Together with their outbuildings from various periods, they represent impressive monuments to the long history of farming and animal husbandry.

And yet, the visitor who travels along old roads with open eyes can trace the history of the settlement of the Finnish countryside and becomes aware of the distinctive character of Finland's provinces. In the fertile landscape of western Finland and Häme, fine farm complexes meet the eye, with sheltered courtyards enclosed by dwellings, sheds, and animal shelters interspersed with trees and hedges. In eastern Finland the structures are spaced out more, and the hilltop villages can be seen from afar. There, our eye rests on tall spruce trees surrounding the yards, magnificent dark, vertical accents against

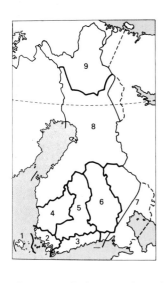

Finland's historical provinces:
1. Ahvenanmaa (Åland)
2. Varsinais-Suomi (Finland Proper)
3. Uusimaa
4. Satakunta
5. Häme
6. Savo
7. Karelia
8. Pohjanmaa (Ostrobothnia)
9. Lappi (Lapland).

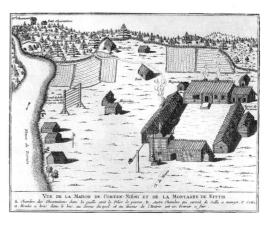

Korteniemi house on the River Tornio, Pello, drawing by the French geographer M. Outhier, 1736-37.

the snow of winter or the soft field hues of summer. In the Ostrobothnian plains, our dominant impression is of splendid courtyards dominated by two-storey farmhouses and of endless expanses dotted with barns. Along the rivers of northern Ostrobothnia, the population thins out as we approach Lapland. Among the rugged fells, we may have an inkling of prehistoric ways of life, though the pine log clusters of modern holiday villages are but a crude carnival version of the handsome dignity of traditional buildings.

The reapportionment of land carried out from the late 18th century on and again in the late 19th century broke up the ancient farming villages in Varsinais-Suomi, Satakunta, and Häme. There, too, farmers built their new homes in the midst of their fields. Close-knit village communities are few and far between today. In Ostrobothnia, the houses are usually built in a row along roads which follow the course of rivers. In the east, settlement was scattered from the start: a village in Savo or Karelia is a group of houses spaced out along a single road or a river or on the side of a hill.

Buildings

Corner-timbering and the associated low pitched roof were common to the oldest buildings of all Finnish provinces. From the late Middle Ages and the following period, only storehouses (*aitta*) remain in Finland. The oldest residential buildings are from the 17th century, larger building complexes from the 18th and 19th centuries. But by comparing a variety of sources, however, we do get some idea about early vernacular architecture and its international sources.

Only the villages of the Skolt Lapps in the far north still contain vertical timber huts (*pistekota*) and twig shelters (*laavu*) like those used in the prehistoric period. The *pistekota* survived longest, even in the south, as a summertime cooking shelter, erected somewhat apart from the main buildings, possibly near the waterfront.

The oldest Finnish dwelling in established agricultural settlements seems to have been the *kota*, a log hut with a squarish ground plan and a low pitched roof supported by joists. The door was at one end; in the middle, at floor level, was an open fireplace. The smoke went out through a vent near the middle of the roof. According to Lars Pettersson, this type of dwelling was already common in Norway and central Sweden as well as among the eastern Finnic peoples of Russia during the late Viking era. It is thought to have been based on the oldest known dwelling type of central Europe, which was in turn developed from the pre-Hellenic Greek *megaron*. In the vernacular architecture of central Europe, the roof pitch later became steeper under

Farmyard of Niemelä croft, Seurasaari.

the influence of Gothic, whereas the low saddle roof remained popular in the north.

The next type of dwelling was the *savupirtti* or *savutupa* ('smoke cottage'), higher than the *kota*, with a masonry stove built next to the door. When the stove was heated, the smoke rose thick to the ceiling, escaping in the Karelia-Savo region through a vent in the ceiling or a flue, in Häme and western Finland through a hatch in the wall. The door was placed functionally high up to keep in the warmth. The interior was divided up in minute detail according to activity. According to Pettersson, the *savupirtti* was particularly well-adapted as a multipurpose dwelling for the semi-permanent lifestyle of the slash-and-burn farmer: it combined lodgings, kitchen, bakery, drying barn, and sauna.

The single-room, pitched-roof *aitta* store-house was adopted in Finland at about the same time as corner-timbering. Farmers built one or more of these structures by the farmyard and used them as sleeping quarters in the summer. *Aittas* with a canopy extending over the entrance are known to have survived in western Finland from as early as the end of the Middle Ages. Occasionally, the logs of the side walls form protruding 'cheeks' framing the canopy. The *aittas* used for storing grain had the tightest structure. In the north, *aittas* raised on a substructure consisting of a post or stilts testify to the problem of keeping stored food out of the

reach of wild animals. In hay barns, a loosely insulated wall of round logs was adequate and functional from the point of view of ventilation.

Niemelän torppa (Niemelä crofter's farm), moved to the open-air museum on Helsinki's Seurasaari island from Konginkangas in central Finland, is an excellent example of the ancient way of life in remote rural areas. This exceptionally well-preserved group of buildings was discovered in 1905 by the painter Gallén and the architect Blomstedt, both folklore enthusiasts. The museum's founder, Professor A.O. Heikel, managed to purchase the buildings and their furnishings in 1909, and made them the principal attraction of the romantic island museum.

The courtyard, flanked by small, grey log buildings, is sheltered but not enclosed. The dwelling consists of a *tupa* (multipurpose room combining the functions of kitchen, dining and living area), a sauna, and a porch. The earliest section, which was in fact initially used as the living area, is the sauna, built in the 1770s of corner-timbered logs that were already old at the time. A separate *savutupa* was later built opposite the old sauna and joined to it with a porch. In its present form, this 'smoke cottage' dates from the mid 19th century. The first *savutupa* in the Niemelä cottage merely had hatches for admitting light, the present building has two glass windows. Built using log joints of various sizes, the building is approximately rectangular.

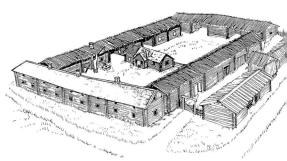

Luhtiaitta storehouse in North Karelia.

North Ostrobothnian farmhouse on the River Kemi.

Antintalo farm, Seurasaari.

The courtyard is based on the terrain contours, with separate, appropriately located log buildings for each of the various functions. The cooking shelter, stables and *aitta* storehouses are nearest to the house, with the cowshed, pigsty and drying barn forming an adjacent 'stock yard'. None of the buildings were painted; all have greyed to a uniform hue.

One of the finest specimens of vernacular architecture is the *luhtiaitta* (storehouse with loft). This is a two-storey building with a partly closed, roofed passage (*sola*) projecting from one of the side walls upstairs. This passage is reached by a staircase entering through its floor. Both storeys contain two or three rooms. The earliest preserved buildings of this type are from the 17th century, the finest specimens are more recent. Many *luhtiaitta* buildings are decorated with exquisite woodwork.

Finnish rural living was transformed in the 16th century by the introduction of a new type of building, the *paritupa* ('double cottage'). This consisted of two multipurpose *tupa* rooms connected by a central hallway. One *tupa* was the family living area, the other was for entertaining

and putting up visitors. Each room had its own open fireplace and glass windows. The hall entrance was fronted by an open porch with a pitched roof. The house could be enlarged by building two bedrooms (*kamari*) on either side of the *tupa* rooms. Pettersson traces the double cottage from the royal demesnes, vicarages and military quarters of sixteenth-century Sweden, which were built to the basic pattern of the elegant residential sections of Renaissance palaces.

Two-storey houses based on Swedish models began to appear in Ostrobothnia in the 18th century. The upper floor, often not used at all, was for display purposes rather than to meet a specific need.

The main building of the Ivars house, moved to Seurasaari from Närpiö in southern Ostrobothnia, was originally built as a vicarage in 1747. The vertical weatherboarding is painted with red ochre, the window frames are white. Yli-Laurosela house in Ilmajoki, built in the mid 19th century, still stands on its original site as a local history museum. The courtyard buildings, preserved intact, testify to the high standard of living in the region.

The form of the farmyard differed from one region to the next. In Karelia and Savo, the irregular placing of buildings was determined by the terrain, roads, river courses, and shorelines. The sauna, drying barn and cooking shelter were usually at some distance from the main

courtyard because of the danger of fire. In western Finland, Ostrobothnia, Uusimaa, and central Finland, a closed plan was favoured: all buildings were placed as regularly as possible around a rectangular courtyard. The closed courtyard clearly arose as a result of Swedish influence. In some places, buildings were grouped around two yards, with housing around the 'man yard', which only the horse could enter from the 'stock yard'.

Antintalo farm was brought to Seurasaari from Säkylä in the province of Satakunta. It forms a completely enclosed courtyard, with buildings side by side around the man yard and stock yard. Between the two yards and facing the main building is a second residential building. The man yard was covered by grass, whereas a magnificent dunghill stood in the middle of the stock yard as a symbol of good housekeeping. The residential buildings are from the nineteenth century, and the older ones have been damaged by fire, but some of the outbuildings date back to the eighteenth century. The affluence of Antintalo farm, with its large main building, a long, extended 'double cottage', stands in marked contrast to the modest way of life represented by Niemelä cottage: the family was a large one and employed many farmhands and servants.

Pertinotsa farm from Suojärvi in the border region of Karelia, also now part of the Seura-saari museum, shows another way to organize a large household. In the Karelian house, the residential quarters and livestock shelters were combined in a single enormous, rectangular log building. The residential section was at one end of the building at second floor level, above the storerooms. The entrance was from a staircase, usually covered and placed on the short side of the building. In front of the living area was a decorative balcony. As the long side of the house ran alongside the road or river, the residential gable end was actually the main facade. At the other end, the livestock shelters were at ground level and the second floor above them was used as a hayloft.

The Karelian house represents the Novgorodian or north Russian house type, which Pettersson has shown to have derived from the mediaeval Byzantine palace. The external walls were not hewn smooth. The imposing effect was enhanced by decorating the balcony at the gable end, the bargeboards of the overhanging eaves and the window frames with fine carvings, and by painting them to contrast with the log walls. According to Pettersson, this type of building was introduced in Karelia in the 17th century and reached its apogee in the mid 19th.

The romanticization of Karelia which inspired Finns at the turn of the century induced architects and painters to explore the villages in the region. Thus plenty of documents, photo-

Bomba House, Suojärvi.

Uhtua, White Sea region of Karelia. Photo: I. K. Inha, 1894.

Gable decorations of Karelian houses. Illustration from Yrjö Blomstedt's and Victor Sucksdorff's book on Karelian architecture.

Fine 18th-century stone barn in Vihti.

---

graphs and drawings of the heyday of this colourful vernacular architecture have been preserved. The most attractive illustrated work is *Karjalaisia rakennuksia ja koristemuotoja* (Karelian buildings and ornamental forms) published 1900 by Yrjö Blomstedt and Victor Sucksdorff. This book was based on an expedition to Russian Karelia in summer 1894. Pertinotsa farm was moved to Seurasaari from Suojärvi in 'Old Finland' in 1939. The region was ceded to the Soviet Union after World War II.

The oldest rural building type is the fieldstone barn, an innovation introduced into agriculture by the physiocratic school of economics during the utilitarian eighteenth century. Tar burning and a budding sawmill industry gave rise to a revaluation of forests as a source of export goods. The Crown sought in various ways to restrict the use of wood in construction in the 18th century. Especially in public building projects, saving wood and more durable con-

struction were the aims. Brick was not available in rural areas, but there was plenty of hard rock. Stone barns were built in slightly different forms in the various regions, depending on natural conditions. The basic principle that they shared was that all manure could be pushed out of hatches in the rear wall. Cows, sheep, pigs and horses had their own pens within the walls of one building.

The fertilization of fields with livestock manure meant a tremendous step forward for grain growing. The large fieldstone barn behind which manure is piled up, ready for spreading onto the fields, is still the most conspicuous monument to the physiocratic movement in the Finnish landscape. An old Finnish proverb states that manure is the king of the fields; the stone barn could be called the temple of manure.

Colours

The origin of the custom of painting wooden buildings in Finland is still unknown. Red ochre has been known from the earliest times: traces of the pigment have been found in Stone Age graves. The first written records of houses painted red, however, are only from the end of the sixteenth century. C.J. Gardberg published a letter by King John III from 1573, containing detailed instructions for the preparation of the red

paint for the Royal Palace in Stockholm. It is generally believed that the practice of painting log walls red was intended to produce an impression similar to that made by the more prestigious brick buildings.

In Finland town halls, churches, and Crown buildings were the first structures to be painted. When Charles XI was due to visit Porvoo in the mid 17th century, the city fathers decided to have the town hall painted red and its roof tarred. Until the end of the century, however, painted buildings were a rarity. Only in the latter half of the eighteenth century did the use of red ochre (a natural pigment containing iron oxide) begin to gain ground in the towns, as the result of a major marketing effort by the Falun mines, which produced it. The most commonly used binders were linseed oil and seal oil. To begin with, only the main facade was painted.

As the use of red ochre became widespread, yellow became the new colour of prestigious architecture. The pigment was developed as an imitation of French sandstone, much in fashion throughout Europe in the 18th century. King Gustavus IV Adolphus sent a letter to several towns in 1803 urging the inhabitants to repaint their houses yellow instead of red, as according to the ruler this was the "most appropriate and gayest" colour.

The most important Finnish buildings, which had previously been red, were gradually repainted in new, lighter colours. The lesser outbuildings, which had previously been left to turn grey, now began to be painted red. Rural areas followed city fashions, but with a considerable lag. The use of red ochre in the Finnish countryside gradually spread north and eastward during the 19th century. Country estates, vicarages, and government buildings naturally followed city fashions most closely, contributing by their example to the increasing popularity of painting. The slowness of the change is illustrated by statistics published by Gardberg about the hillside villages of the eastern parts of Kajaani rural municipality: in 1949, over 80 per cent of the houses were still unpainted. Of the houses that were painted, more than 90 per cent were red, even though a fairly wide range of colours was available by that time. Gardberg draws an interesting conclusion: "Far on our eastern border, the same development could be observed quite recently which had begun long ago, perhaps even during the late Gothic period in the 15th century."

In Lapland one still hears talk of "the painted villages of the South". The painting of houses was never established practice in the most northerly vernacular architecture. There untreated log buildings are very durable: the surface becomes weathered and grey, but rot does not penetrate deep into the wood in the cold climate.

Porvoo Cathedral towers above the historic town.

The Middle Ages and the sixteenth century

Castles

The castles built in Finland in the Middle Ages tell the tale of how the King of Sweden claimed lands for the crown and strengthened his position in the eastern provinces. Secular and ecclesiastical rule were separated, and the laity strengthened its hold on power as the Middle Ages drew to an end. The first administrative units were castle fiefs; the province also became an established concept. The feudal lords initially built castles solely for military purposes, but later also to serve the growing needs of an aristocratic lifestyle. The rule of Gustavus Vasa (1523–60) brought the era of feudalism to an end: from then on, the castles were commanded by governors appointed by the King.

Only two mediaeval castles, Vanhalinna in Lieto and Hakoinen in Janakkala, were built on the sites of prehistoric fortifications. Most of the ninety-odd primitive forts lost their significance as the country was reorganized under the Swedish crown. All in all, the crown possessions in Finland in the Middle Ages amounted to some ten castles and fortified manors. The most important castles, both for administrative and defensive purposes, were those of Turku, Häme, Viipuri, and Olavinlinna.

In 1280, Carolus Gustavi was appointed governor of Finland, and Turku Castle was built at the mouth of the River Aura, evidently as his

Aerial photograph of Turku Castle, 1927.

residence. Under Duke Valdemar in the 1310s the simple military camp was enlarged into a fortress. The construction of the castles of Hakoinen and Häme on the initiative of Birger Jarl established the province of Häme as the seat of government in the mid 13th century. Bo Jonsson Grip enlarged several castles, building the stone stronghold of Kastelholma at the site of an old fortified camp in the Åland Islands and the castle of Raasepori in Uusimaa. Karl Knutsson Bonde built the castle of Viipuri in the 1440s, Erik Axelsson Tott Olavinlinna Castle in 1475.

All fortresses of the Crown were built in stages to adjust to changing situations, needs, and means. Later additions, removals, alterations, and renovations – most recently a series of thoroughgoing restorations completed in the 1980s – all had a significant impact on the architecture of the castles. The incidental visitor has difficulty tracing the different building periods. In many cases, even experts disagree about the dating of old strata hidden under later construction or entirely destroyed. The following account, based mainly on C.J. Gardberg, is confined to the principal events in the history of the largest castles up to the sixteenth century.

The first phase of Turku Castle was a greystone castellum, or fortified camp, measuring 65 x 30 metres and built in the 1280s on an island at the mouth of the river Aura. The walls were some nine metres high and pierced on each side by a gate; at the short ends, the gates were flanked by projecting towers. The first gateway, later vaulted over to make part of the cellar, has been preserved at the ground floor of the present castle. The attractive narrow greystone masonry of the barrel vault indicates that the masons came from Gotland.

Enlargement got under way no later than the 1310s, under Duke Valdemar. The large courtyard was divided with a transverse wall into a bailey and keep, the west side becoming the keep. The east tower guarded the only gate. The towers and walls were raised. The west tower became a five-storey residence topped with battlements. A three-storey hall was built on the north side of the dividing wall, containing the main living quarters reserved for the king or duke. This building phase was modelled on German castles.

The third and most important mediaeval construction phase of Turku Castle took place around 1400. Three-storey wing buildings of equal height were added to all four sides, further reducing the width of the ward divided by the transverse wall. The most important rooms were built into the north wing: the royal hall, with two aisles and high groin vaults; and the square chapel later known as the Nuns' Chapel, with four stellar vaults. With some forty rooms, the castle was now one of the largest in northern Europe.

The fourth building phase has been dated on

*Häme Castle.
Ornamental
brickwork of the
northeast wing's
courtyard wall.*

heraldic evidence to the 1480s, during the regency of Sten Sture the Elder. The east tower was raised and the 'Sture Church' was built.

The ascent of Gustavus Vasa to the throne in 1523 also marked the beginning of a new era for Turku Castle. The new plans were adjusted to the needs of firearms development and the culture of a Continental Renaissance court. The interiors of the mediaeval castle, however, were never rebuilt in a single, unified style. Separate entrances led from the ward to the various suites via staircases and passageways. The Middle Ages prepared for war by building windows only on the ward side and by furnishing each of the wings with battlements above the dwellings.

With the introduction of cannon, the defences had to be moved down to ground level to protect the walls. Housing and defence works became separate architectural assignments. Turku Castle was not innovative in the development of earthworks and other newfangled fortifications. During the governorship of Gustavus Vasa's son John in the mid 16th century the building developed into a residential castle unique in Finland; in fact it was the country's first Renaissance palace.

The first concession to comfort was the angle tower, built at the northeast corner of the keep in 1549–50 with a quadrilateral staircase punctuated by landings for resting. This Renaissance feature differed drastically from the all-but-

impassable, steep and narrow stairs of mediaeval castles, and permitted well-dressed people to proceed in a dignified manner from one storey to the next. The Renaissance staircase had originated in Italy, and probably came to Sweden via France, the Netherlands, and Denmark: the first one in Stockholm Castle was built 1543.

The most significant alterations and enlargements were commissioned by John, made Duke of Finland in 1556. He married Catherine Jagellonica, the sister of the king of Poland, in 1562, thus linking remote Turku closely with the courts of Europe – Catherine's mother was Bona Sforza, princess of Milan.

The wall that had divided the mediaeval fortress in two was pulled down, creating a single keep. Old rooms were combined and the battlements above the south and north wings were replaced by new, spacious halls. A quadrilateral tower was built in the middle of the courtyard with a wide staircase connecting with all levels of the south wing. Access to the north wing was over either of two wooden bridges, one on top of the other. The new storey in the north wing was entered by way of a central hallway flanked by the duke's and duchess's apartments, each consisting of a salon and a bedchamber. The new storey had large glazed windows both on the courtyard side and in the outside wall. The straight ceilings had ingeniously carved wood panelling. The lower parts of the walls in the

Viipuri Castle before the wars.

main halls were also panelled; above them hung Flemish tapestries. The coherent series of well-lit halls can be compared with the contemporaneous royal suite in Vadstena Castle.

In their present state, the halls reflect the austere principles observed in restoration: as no original panelling or furniture remained, these were replaced by designs which merely hint at the original.

Once the mediaeval castle had been unified as a single keep, a new, enclosed bailey was built on the east side in the 16th century. Its gate was moved in 1549 from the river side to the middle of the east wall, producing a fairly symmetrical building 120 metres long. The round tower in the southeast corner was built 1568–74. The bailey wings were not completed until the 1580s.

According to Knut Drake, Häme Castle was founded on an island in Lake Vanajavesi in the late 1260s. The first structure was a square (33 x 33 metres) fortified camp with a deep moat and walls of massive greystone seven metres high.

Ten rooms or so were built within the encircling wall during the 13th century. The main room is the oldest preserved ceremonial hall in Finland. The residential castle proper developed during the early 14th century. The projecting Cock Tower was built over the southwest wall. With a square plan and a gate at second-floor level, it contained living quarters in the manner of similar structures on the Continent.

Construction of Häme Castle resumed after the Swedish-Russian peace treaty of Pähkinäsaari (1323). Brick, a very rare building material in Finland at the time, was now used for the facades and detailing. The use of brick construction and the Gothic architectural idiom were due to the influence of the Teutonic Knights. Planning and supervision were evidently in the hands of foreigners, whereas the bricks were made and laid by local labour. Brick provided opportunities for more refined spatial arrangements and facade ornament. The decoration of the courtyard walls is unique in Finland.

The brick castle had reached its final height by the mid 15th century, though the north and west towers were built later. The advent of firearms made it necessary to extend the defence lines farther out from the main castle; the old castle was surrounded with outworks.

As the land surrounding the castle dried out, construction in the following centuries centred on the outer fortifications. A round gun turret, or roundel, was built at the east corner of the outworks. All flanks could be controlled from the loopholes of the two towers.

The restoration of Häme Castle from 1950 to 1979 retrieved as much as possible of the oldest history of the complex, which had been greatly damaged by various disasters and long use as a prison. The Gothic vaults of the mediaeval royal hall were reconstructed.

Olavinlinna Castle in Savonlinna.

Viipuri Castle, located in territory ceded to the Soviet Union after the last war, celebrated its 700th anniversary in summer 1993. The circumstances of its founding are not known, but during the third Finnish crusade in 1293, the Swedes founded the fortress at the mouth of the river Vuoksi to strengthen their hegemony over Novgorod in the region. The Swedish *Eriks krönika* (Chronicle of Erik) records that the crusaders "built a castle at the edge where Christian land ends and heathen land begins".

Built on an island in the shape of an irregular rectangle, the first castle was a fortified camp of grey granite three or four storeys high. It contained the projecting Tower of St. Olof. Greystone walls surrounded the castle courtyard east of the tower; wooden houses were gradually erected against the encircling wall. According to Gardberg, the extent of later enlargements, with wings built inside the walls, was thus already determined by the end of the 13th century. The last mediaeval construction phase was during the governorship of Karl Knutsson Bonde from 1442 to 1448. At this time, the castle was enlarged and furnished in a manner appropriate for holding court. The work was continued by Erik Axelsson Tott, who also built the walls and towers that guarded the mediaeval town.

Olavinlinna Castle is located on a rocky islet in the Kyrönsalmi straits, a major crossing of waterways. Erik Axelsson Tott founded the castle in 1475 to protect the eastern border regions from the growing power of the Grand Duchy of Muscovy in the Novgorod region.

Mediaeval Olavinlinna consisted of a three-towered keep and east outworks encircled by a wall fortified by either two or three towers. The two towers of the keep, connected by walls some 13 metres high, rose from the highest point of the island's rocky ridge. The living quarters and storerooms were in wing buildings within the walls. The towers also contained dwellings. A bridge from the main gate crossed the straits to Tallisaari island. All of the mediaeval buildings were built of local greystone.

Olavinlinna was the first castle in Scandinavia to be designed specifically for the use of firearms. All of the towers were round. The archives show that sixteen foreign stonemasons worked there, including master craftsmen from Tallinn and Gotland, possibly also from Russia. The architecture is closely related to that of Baltic castles, with Italian and Balkan influences transmitted by craftsmen who had moved to Russia from these regions.

During the reign of Gustavus Vasa, the towers of the keep were raised with brick walls. Renovation of the outworks began after the Swedish-Russian war of 1555–57 and continued until the 1610s. A roundel known as the 'Fat Tower' was built in the southeast corner, the tall Kijl Tower at the east end of the north wall.

Jomala Church.

Hammarland Church from the soutwest.

Nousiainen Church.

Olavinlinna surrendered to the Russians in 1714 during the Great Northern War after suffering heavy damage. In the Peace of Turku in 1743, the castle remained in Russian territory. Its present appearance is largely the result of repairs and renovation undertaken by the Russians in the 1790s. Antero Sinisalo has shown that attention was already paid to the castle's architectural features at this early time. After the War of Finland (1808–09), the castle reverted to Finland, but its significance to the country's defence was negligible.

The restoration of Olavinlinna between 1961 and 1975 is an interesting chapter in the management of Finland's architectural heritage. Proud and sculpturesque on its island site, the castle still makes an exceptionally emotional appeal to scholars and casual visitors alike.

Churches

Through the efforts of the Catholic Church, Christianity advanced in Scandinavia in the 12th century side by side with efforts to strengthen monarchic rule. This was a general European political trend. Several families vied for power in Sweden; many a brief reign came to a violent end.

Our knowledge of the crusades to Finland is largely based on legend, which the church and later generations of rulers exploited to strengthen their position. The legend of how King Erik converted the Finns during a single crusade in 1155 was propagated by the diocese of Uppsala cathedral with the support of the ruling family, the Folkungas. Erik was a real person, the founder of a new dynasty. He was killed in the 1190s and canonized soon thereafter.

The ship of the first crusade came to land somewhere in Varsinais-Suomi. According to legend, the English-born Bishop Henry of Uppsala stayed with a small army to convert the heathen Finns and to set up a new church. He was active in Kokemäki, Nousiainen, and in Köyliö, where the farmer Lalli killed him in January 1156. Modern scholars believe that the region had already quietly converted to Christianity by this time: both the Christian-type graves from the period and signs of earlier wooden churches suggest this. Lalli may have been angered by the church levies.

Mediaeval sources do not tell us where Henry set up his first bishopric; the fact that he was buried in Nousiainen, however, suggests that this was the see.

Construction of churches began in Finland in the 12th century and continued apace until the early decades of the 16th century. Excavations have yielded scant information about the earliest wooden churches, but the fairly uniform architectural plans of the greystone churches suggest that the basic type was already in use in the earliest Christian phase. The first churches, like the humble village churches and chapels built later, differed little from the older corner-timbered dwellings of the Finns.

The surviving seventy-three stone churches and fifteen stone sacristies built in connection with wooden churches bear a strong family resemblance: a rectangular nave built of large greystone blocks, with a sacristy on the north side and a porch on the south side. The high pitched roofs are often clad with tarred shingles. The only conspicuous features of international Gothic are the high roofs, the brick profiles of door and window openings, and the brick ornamentation of some gable ends.

Most of the churches are built to a three-aisle hall plan, but impressive spatial effects were also obtained with vaulted single-aisle and two-aisle interiors. The fresco decoration of vaults and walls, quite rich at times, complements the elegantly primitive architecture.

Mediaeval churches were built, enlarged, completed and renovated by gradual phases. Each church has its own architectural strata; the more important the church, the more complex its history. For a coherent picture of the development of Finnish architecture in the Middle Ages, one would have to examine the churches phase by phase, returning to each building several times. Instead, we shall proceed like the casual tourist from one region to the next, picking out a variety of impressive overall views.

The earliest group of stone churches in Finland consists of eleven red granite churches in the Åland archipelago. Scholars still disagree about their age, but it seems probable that the first churches were built in Åland in the 13th century, mainly based on models in Östergötland and Gotland. Traces of even older wooden churches have been found in the foundations.

One of the oldest is St. Olof's Church in Jomala, originally a simple, compact structure consisting of a square nave with a sturdy, somewhat narrower tower at the far end and fronted by a chancel as wide as the tower and lower than the nave.

According to Gardberg, the churches of Saltvik, Sund, and Lemland were built between 1280 and 1300 to simple, rectangular hall plans. The nave of the church of Lemland was always covered by a flat wooden roof. Sund Church was vaulted to a two-aisle plan in the 15th century in a style imported from Tallinn. Robust towers were later built at the west ends of the aisles, obviously for defensive purposes.

Turku Cathedral

Pietari Kemiöläinen raised Finland's highest church vaults over the nave of Turku Cathedral.

Mynämäki Church.

Sauvo Church.

The tower of Hammarland Church was built on the south side of the west part of the main nave. The interior, too, is unusual, consisting as it does of two vaulted squares. The vaults, built of unhewn stone, are very early.

The early 14th century church of Eckerö originally had a rectangular interior. The tower at the west end, as wide as the nave, was added later. The vaults in Finström Church, built of unhewn stone and borne by massive pillars, produce an extraordinary primitive spatial impact; yet the vaults, perhaps the whole interior, were probably built as late as the 15th century.

Twenty-three parish churches of stone were built in Varsinais-Suomi in the Middle Ages, most of them on the site of an earlier wooden church. According to Gardberg, the sacristy is older than the nave in twenty of these churches.

The church of Nousiainen, built in the late 13th century and consecrated to Bishop Henry, was the first stone church to be completed on the Finnish mainland. Because of its exceptional function, it had a pentagonal chancel narrower than the nave. The walls were built of unhewn stone to window height and of brick from there up. The fine brick masonry of the pointed arches suggests a connection with the builders of Sweden's Lake Mälar region. The interior was vaulted with three aisles in the 1370s.

The eventful history of Turku Cathedral goes back to the 1250s, when German merchants built a wooden church for the needs of their settlement on Unikankare hill. The foundations of a small stone sacristy attached to the first church have been discovered under the floor of the present sacristy.

A cathedral chapter was established in Turku in 1276, and the sanctuary was converted by the year 1300 into a hall church with a brick exterior and a pentagonal chancel narrower than the nave. This chancel, like the similar one at Nousiainen, was commissioned by Bishop John I from Sigtuna in the Mälar valley, and presumably built by masters brought by the bishop from his home region.

A west tower and two porches were added to this church before it burned down in a raid by the Novgorodians in 1318. The church was then rebuilt with three vaulted aisles in the manner of Tallinn.

Two lines of chapels, along the north and south walls, enhance the spaciousness of the in-

terior. The first individual chapels were built during the 14th century; the increasing worship of saints prompted the enlargement a hundred years later. The tower was raised, the sacristy enlarged and raised. The following building phase raised Turku Cathedral into a magnificent category of its own in the history of Finnish architecture. The nave was enlarged along the previous ring of chapels and furnished with high groin vaults in 1466, turning it into a high basilica. The clerestory windows of the central nave cast an even light on the interior. The demanding project was directed by the Finnish master builder Pietari Kemiöläinen. The west tower may have been raised to its final height at this time. This made Turku Cathedral the dominant feature in the townscape, in the manner of the fine town churches in northern Germany and Tallinn.

The church reached its final length in 1471, when the octagonal All Saints' Chapel was completed as an extension to the chancel. Later alterations were undertaken after fires; after the Reformation, the interiors were refurbished for the needs of the new Lutheran doctrine, and after the disastrous fire of 1827 C.L. Engel designed a Neo-Gothic spire for the tower.

The history of the churches in the vicinity of Turku is in many ways connected with that of the cathedral. Its forms are repeated in the churches of Nousiainen, Mynämäki, Vehmaa, and Taivassalo. Probably the masters who had been brought to Turku also worked in these parishes. The three-aisle hall church of Mynämäki, one of the largest mediaeval churches in Finland, was vaulted before 1350 in the style of the first vaulted cathedral.

The churches of Raisio and Parainen differ from those discussed above. The long, narrow Raisio Church is reminiscent in form of the Uppland region in Sweden. Parainen Church is of the pseudobasilican type, with three high aisles, the vaulting of the central aisle being higher than that of the side aisles. Its elegant brickwork suggests that construction was supervised by the same masters from northern Germany who built the new main chancel in Turku Cathedral.

The skilfully made vaults of the churches of Sauvo, Kemiö, Perniö and Tenhola were built by Pietari Kemiöläinen, the master responsible for the high vaults of Turku Cathedral.

The first stone churches in Satakunta and Häme were built in the 14th century. Ulvila Church has a long, narrow floor plan (28.5 x 11 metres), as do those of Tyrvää and Huittinen; Karkku Church is wider.

No new churches were built in Satakunta during the first half of the fifteenth century. Not until Maunu Särkilahti was bishop (1489–1500) were the churches of Ulvila and Huittinen vaulted and fitted with ornamental brick gables; an entirely new church was built in Lempäälä. The

Tyrvää Church.

The brick church of Hattula.

Ring vaults in Hollola Church.

vaulting of Ulvila Church is closely related to those of churches in Sweden's Uppland and Norrland provinces. Flanked by massive wall pillars, the nave is the only one of its kind in Finland. St. Olof's Church in Tyrvää has the finest gable decorations in all Satakunta.

In Häme, Hattula Church (built c. 1370–1420) is Finland's only mediaeval church to have been built entirely of brick. The choice of material is believed to have been dictated by the proximity of Häme Castle. The facade brickwork is elegantly ornamental. The three-aisle nave is dominated by the abundant decorative frescoes painted in the 16th century.

The importance of the province of Häme increased towards the end of the fifteenth century. The region was part of the fief of the powerful Erik Axelsson Tott of Viipuri. The fact that no less than twelve stone churches were built there in the period is interpreted by Antero Sinisalo almost as a sign of a crusading spirit. The oldest and architecturally most significant of these churches is in Hollola, an ancient regional centre. St. Mary's in Hollola is the third largest of all mediaeval parish churches in Finland. Some of the furnishings of the two-aisled church's large chancel have been preserved, notably parts of the exquisitely carved rood screen and choir loft. Hollola Church has 'ring vaults', quadripartite stellar vaults, with ring patterns formed at all intersections of ribs. The two-

aisled plan seems to have been a novelty introduced from the Danish islands or the southern Baltic; the ring vaults were probably a borrowing from Sweden's Södermanland region. Sinisalo believes that the master builders were the same international crew who worked in Viipuri and on the castles of Olavinlinna and Häme.

The church of Vanaja, with three large ring vaults, is closely related to that of Hollola. The churches of Sääksmäki, Lammi and Hauho, and the vestry of Tuulos Church, belong to the same family. The churches of Sysmä, Pälkäne and Janakkala were built during the last surge of mediaeval building in the late 15th and early 16th centuries. Later changes and additions in many of the churches of Häme have been so drastic that the traveller can safely concentrate on Hattula and Hollola.

The busy period of church construction that began in the late 15th century is usually treated separately in descriptions of Finnish architectural history. The primacy of the church and the power of the bishops were established, and the dioceses were efficiently organized. Many bishops sought purposefully to initiate the construction of new churches and to improve old ones. Plenty of master builders versed in the complexities of vaulting techniques were available. Monasteries and nunneries founded in the early 15th century added significant impulses to architecture. There was a Dominican friary in Turku,

Profuse frescoes dominate the interior of Lohja Church.

West gable end of Pernaja Church, drawing by Carolus Lindberg.

Pernaja Church.

Franciscan friaries in Viipuri, Rauma, and Kökar, and a convent of the order of St. Bridget (Birgitta) in Naantali.

Construction was liveliest in southern Finland and Häme. The churches from this period can be immediately recognized by the fine brickwork gable ornamentation. The three-aisled interiors usually had simple groin vaults for the aisles and an ornamental stellar vault for the nave; in the altar end this was often further highlighted by especially decorative forms.

The first stone churches in Uusimaa were built in Tenhola, Karjaa, Inkoo, Lohja, Kirkkonummi and Porvoo. The churches of Helsinki parish, Pohja, Siuntio, Espoo, Vihti, Sipoo, Pernaja and Pyhtää are somewhat younger. Many of these parishes were originally dependent on larger mother parishes, and did not build churches until they became 'independent'. Most of the stone churches in Uusimaa were built in the 15th century, though parts of the walls of the churches of Kirkkonummi, Inkoo and Porvoo go back to the 13th century.

The large church of Lohja, like the church of Hattula, is known best for its magnificent frescoes. The vaults and gable brickwork have been dated back to the last quarter of the fifteenth century, the paintings to the era of Finland's last Catholic bishop, Arvid Kurki (1510–22).

The history of the present cathedral of Porvoo goes back to the 13th century; the most extensive enlargement took place during the late Gothic period. Most of the brick-ribbed vaults of this three-aisle basilican church were rebuilt after a fire in the 18th century, but an eight-ribbed stellar vault preserved in the chancel is one of the earliest of its kind in Finland.

The ornamental brick gables of Porvoo cathedral, on a prominent hilltop site, still dominate the historic townscape. The decorative field, consisting of a recessed horizontal band, a row of rings and large cruciform niches, was much imitated throughout Uusimaa and Varsinais-Suomi; it is possible that the same masons produced similar gables for different churches. The west ends of the churches of Sipoo, Pyhtää, Pernaja, Helsinki parish, and Perniö, at any rate, bear considerable resemblance to the Porvoo composition. Since these churches also had eight-pointed stellar vaults, scholars have concluded that the vaults and gable decoration were the work of the same masters.

Carsten Nübuhr, who directed the enlargement of Porvoo Church, was also in charge of the vaulting and gable construction in the 1450s of the church of Pernaja (built in the 1390s). The many funeral coats of arms from later centuries, telling the story of the aristocratic families of eastern Uusimaa, add a pleasing touch to the well-preserved interior.

The oldest stone churches of Ostrobothnia (Pohjanmaa) – those of Mustasaari, Pietarsaari

parish, and Isokyrö – were built before 1450. With their long, narrow plan, these churches are closely related to the architecture of Swedish Norrland across the Gulf of Bothnia. Only the church of Isokyrö has retained its mediaeval form; Mustasaari Church is in ruins, and Pietarsaari parish church was altered to a cruciform plan in the 18th century; the latter church, however, is the only one to have preserved the narrow west tower typical of the region, though it was later raised and recently received a new roofing after a fire in 1985.

The large church of Isokyrö never had a tower. The oldest part is the sacristy, which dates from the 14th century. The nave has a traditional wooden barrel vault. After the Reformation of the 16th century, the church was embellished with extensive frescoes. According to Riitta Pylkkänen, some of the paintings, which are reminiscent of Renaissance tapestries, were inspired by the Biblia Pauperum, the Bible for the uneducated poor.

The last Ostrobothnian churches date from the period after the war with Russia in the 1490s, and have no decorative brick gables. Of the churches of Närpiö, Kaarlela, Alatornio, and Kemi, only Kemi Church has kept its mediaeval garb.

The Church of Sweden broke off all relations with Rome in 1524. Gustavus Vasa became head of the national church, and Sweden the first western state to repudiate the Catholic Church during the Reformation. The king began to undermine the position of the church by levying taxes and fees. No more new churches were built, and the days of prosperity were over for the old ones, too.

Towns

There were only six towns in Finland at the close of the Middle Ages: Turku and Viipuri acquired town rights before the year 1300, Porvoo and Ulvila in the mid 14th century, and Rauma and Naantali in the 1440s. None of these have the romantic mazes of winding streets and closely built little houses that have been tourist attractions in central Europe since the end of the nineteenth century. Finland's mediaeval towns were small, and their modest wooden houses have burned down many times over the centuries. Only in Viipuri have a handful of small mediaeval stone houses been preserved. Ulvila, founded on the banks of the river Kokemäenjoki, has disappeared entirely: the former seaport lost its significance when the coastal uplift left it far inland.

The first Turku, burned down by the Novgorodians in 1318, was built around the church. C.J. Gardberg has shown that the town was rebuilt after the 1320s in imitation of Danzig. An oblong square was laid out on the south

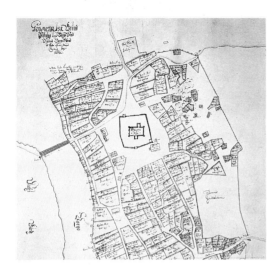

Surveyor's plan drawing of Porvoo town, 1696.

side of the church, with the town hall at the upper end and a river crossing at the lower end; a bridge was built in the early 15th century. The main coastal road from Viipuri and the Häme 'ox road' from Häme Castle met at the town hall square. The crossing of the river Aura provided a connection from these roads to the castle, the sea route to Åland, and on to Stockholm.

The devastating fire of 1827 and the Neoclassical urban ideal removed the last vestiges of the Middle Ages in the historical centre of Turku, leaving the church in splendid isolation. Among the broad streets, widened for the needs of increasing traffic, the mediaeval cathedral now stands, all but forgotten, in the middle of a roundabout. The outline of the old town hall square can still be distinguished in the row of nineteenth-century houses, and the enormous deciduous trees of Porthan park hint at the depth of the strata of civilization underneath.

The castle of Viipuri, built by Tyrgils Knutsson, guarded the trade route of the east. The town was built on a peninsula east of the island on which the castle stood. Dominican and Franciscan monasteries lent the small frontier outpost special significance in the 14th and 15th centuries. Viipuri was the only mediaeval Finnish town to have been completely encircled by a defensive wall. Built by Erik Axelsson Tott in the 1470s, the wall was guarded by nearly a dozen towers. The castle and town walls were

strengthened in the 16th century. The renowned Round Tower, or *Karjaportintorni* (Cattle Gate Tower), dates from this period.

The first town of Porvoo sprang up around the church, built at an important intersection of roads from all directions by the river Porvoo. According to Gardberg, the square on the north side of the church is as old as the building itself. A town hall was later erected nearer the river with a square of its own. Steep, narrow alleys and a row of riverbank storehouses lend old Porvoo a highly individual flavour. Although repeated fires destroyed all residential buildings erected before 1760, the setting still has something of a mediaeval atmosphere, with its street network following the rivercourse and hilly terrain. The long, narrow plots extend from one street to the next, by the river right down to the waterfront. The setting has been threatened by various renovation projects over the last century. Preservation was first advocated by the Swedish artist Louis Sparre, who delivered a lecture in 1898 on the aesthetic values of the mediaeval town and founded a popular movement for saving Porvoo.

The town of Rauma started out as a trading place in the 14th century; a Franciscan monastery was founded there in the following century. Next to the town church (built in the early 15th century) was a trading place, the present-day fish market. Most of the houses clustered

Old Rauma in the early 1970s.

around this site. Although the Rauma street network shows some mediaeval irregularity, Markus Hiekkanen has demonstrated that efforts to clarify the town plan by opening up straight streets were made from the 17th century on. The straight Kuninkaankatu from the eastern toll gate to the market square dates from the 17th century.

UNESCO has included the old town of Rauma in its cultural heritage list because of the unique unity of its townscape. This idyll, too, was saved only because fiery artists and architects rose up to oppose a regular grid plan drawn up at the end of the nineteenth century. The townspeople's own initiative and sensible renovation policies have steered Rauma's development in an unusually successful way.

Naantali was founded by royal decree to support the Brigittine nunnery of Vallis Gratiae: the convent needed trade and pilgrims needed accommodation. The town plan was simple: the main street led inland from the inlet south of the convent, continuing from where settlement ended as the highway to Turku. On both sides of this thoroughfare were houses and short cross streets. The only parts left of the oldest buildings in Naantali, as in Rauma, are the remains of mediaeval brick cellars.

Gustavus Vasa systematically sought to develop Finland's towns. He concentrated all trading in them, denying farmers the right to engage in independent overseas trade. The king founded Tammisaari in 1546 and Helsinki at the mouth of the river Vantaa in 1550. Helsinki was planned as a rival trading port to Tallinn, but the forcibly resettled citizens of Ulvila, Rauma, Porvoo and Tammisaari kept absconding to their former domiciles, and the grandiose plans for the new town miscarried. The people moved from Tammisaari were permitted to return home in 1556. Today Tammisaari boasts a lovely old town on Barcken peninsula, with the oldest houses dating back to the 18th century.

The urban projects of Gustavus's son John III fared no better. The renovation of Turku never took place; Pori became no more than a small, irregular hamlet; plans for the towns of Espoo and Tornio never got off the ground. John did have some success in promoting the construction of stone houses in Viipuri. The new town district of Valli was built to the east of the mediaeval town wall and surrounded by a system of bastions; John forbade the building of inferior streets such as those in the old town. The precise extent to which these plans were implemented, however, is not known.

Louhisaari Manor, Askainen.

The seventeenth century

Sweden's brief period of glory as a major power began with the coronation of King Gustavus II Adolphus in 1611. From then until the reign of Charles XII (1697–1718) and the Great Northern War (1700–1721), Sweden waged a series of successful wars on the Continent and ranked as a European superpower – albeit the smallest one.

The reign of the highly cultivated Gustavus Adolphus was a time of rapid cultural, administrative, and economic development in Finland, too. Local government was reinforced in various ways; a particulary significant step was the appointment of the first Governor-General of Finland in 1623. New institutions with a long-term impact were the Turku Court of Appeal, founded in 1623, and the Turku Academy (1640).

The towns were entrusted with the development of trade. A hierarchic network of staple towns and inland towns was set up in Finland: foreign trade was the main task of the staples, trade with the farmers that of the inland towns.

During Sweden's years as a major power, its trade policy, later named mercantilism, was aimed at increasing State revenue: this was necessary to finance war. Mining and the export trade brought immediate gains, therefore they were developed throughout the realm, including Finland. Though no major ore deposits were discovered in Finland despite all efforts, many ironworks were established, and some of them developed into distinctive communities. The

Some streets in Raahe still hint at the original 17th-century town plan.

Map of Finnish towns founded in the 17th century and before.

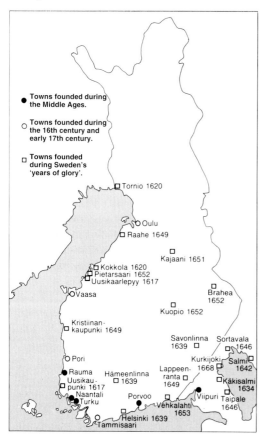

Towns founded during the Middle Ages.

Towns founded during the 16th century and early 17th century.

Towns founded during Sweden's 'years of glory'.

Tornio 1620

Oulu
Raahe 1649

Kajaani 1651

Kokkola 1620
Pietarsaari 1652
Uusikaarlepyy 1617

Vaasa

Brahea
1652

Kuopio 1652

Kristiinan-
kaupunki 1649

Savonlinna   Sortavala
1639   1646

Pori

Kurkijoki   Salmi
Lappeen-   1668   1642
ranta
1649   Käkisalmi
                  1634

Rauma   Hämeenlinna
Uusikau-   1639
punki 1617   Viipuri   Taipale
Naantali   Porvoo   1646
Turku
                  Vehkalahti
                  1653
Helsinki 1639
Tammisaari

Mustio works started operation in 1617, that of Antskog soon after. In the 1640s, another iron-works was established at Pinjainen (Billnäs) in the municipality of Pohja, and a smelting works and forge at Fagervik in Inkoo.

The power of the nobility grew during the reign of Gustavus Adolphus and his successor, Queen Christina. The wealth of the aristocracy before the 'reduction' (revocation of powers) carried out by Charles XI in the 1680s is reflected in a handful of churches and country estates built in Finland during the period, and particularly in the church furnishings. By far the finest of the manor houses were Louhisaari, built in Askainen by the Fleming family in the 1650s, and Sarvilahti, built in Pernaja by the Creutz family some twenty years later. These handsome, three-storey stone buildings were the northernmost examples of Dutch Baroque Classicism. The Louhisaari estate includes a small stone church of harmonious proportions built just before the manor house in 1653; the chancel features a 'pew of the gentry' for the Fleming family.

As a result of lively international contacts, the stylistic ideals of the Baroque and its abundance of forms were gradually adopted from the Mediterranean countries and central Europe, although it took time even for the more restrained style of the Renaissance to take root. The guild system spread to Finland in the 1620s.

Kokkola pedagogium.

All building in towns was based on regular grid plans. The cruciform church was introduced as an alternative to the traditional basilican type.

Towns

The new profession of surveyor was needed to make it possible to build towns to a regular plan. Henrik Lilius, whose studies the present account is based on, discovered that in 1628, the year that the Swedish geodetic society was founded, the surveyor Anders Bure was commissioned to survey all the towns in the realm in order to give the King an idea of their condition and to decide how to bring order to them. New towns were founded and old ones replanned according to royal instructions. The surveyors staked out future streets, blocks and plots in the terrain before construction; the plans were thus drawn up on site, not at the drawing board.

Four new towns were established along the Gulf of Bothnia during the reign of Gustavus II Adolphus: Uusikaupunki in 1617, Uusikaarlepyy, Kokkola and Tornio in 1620. The first town plans were grids of streets of standard width surveyed along the shoreline. Single-storey wooden houses were built on the small plots, with both the short and long wall facing a street. Lilius calls this period the age of beginning regularity. Dutch town planning ideas prevailed.

Stricter regularity and a richer urban structure were achieved when Per Brahe was Governor-General of Finland from 1637 to 1641 and 1648 to 1653. By this time, French and Italian town planning theory had a direct influence. This was a period of urban development quite unique in Finnish history: the number of towns rose between 1617 and 1688 from eleven to thirty. They remained small, however: only Turku and Viipuri had a population of more than one thousand, most of the other towns had from two hundred to five hundred inhabitants. Less than three per cent of the country's population lived in towns.

Among the first towns established under Per Brahe were Hämeenlinna and Savonlinna. He also moved Helsinki, withering on its original site at the mouth of the river Vantaa, to its present site on Vironniemi peninsula. Within his own barony, Brahe founded Kajaani in 1651. His main planners were two surveyors, Anders Torstenson and Claes Claesson.

The town planning principles of the seventeenth century are most clearly reflected today in the towns of Ostrobothnia. The grid plans are strictly rectangular and all streets of equal width. The blocks are rectangular or square, and fit in two rows of plots. Terrain contours were ignored; the shoreline was only important in that it provided a harbour. Many towns were set apart from the countryside by a toll gate, accen-

Luoto Church at Pyhämaa, interior and exterior.

Watercolour by Armas Lindgren of the Saloinen Church interior, 1896.

Structural drawing of a block pillar, Eero Pettersson.

tuating their closed form and character.

As a rule, the single-storey, pitched-roof houses in Per Brahe's towns were built with the long wall facing the street. Plank fences were an extension of the walls as the street border. The fences had gates opening into the courtyard; the houses could only be entered from the courtyard. Thus the public and private domain were kept strictly separate. Outbuildings were located in the yard, turning their back on similar buildings on the neighbouring plot. The garden and vegetable patch were between the house and the outbuildings. The streetscape was uniform. A few of the streets of Raahe, Kokkola and Kristiinankaupunki still recapture this ideal, if one remembers that the houses were neither boarded nor painted with light colours in the seventeenth century; the streetscape must have been uniformly grey.

At the centre of the grid towns of Per Brahe's time was the market square. Lilius has divided the market squares of the period into four categories: the square with open corners, the square with closed corners, the square formed by leaving parts of two opposing blocks unbuilt, and the square with incomplete corners. The town hall was built on one side of the market square, the location of all trade.

Most towns built a town hall during the 17th century, and other public construction also stepped up despite the objections of the burghers. Many of the town halls were fine two-storey buildings embellished with a clock tower, but they have all been destroyed. Of the many school buildings, only the two-storey elementary school, or *pedagogium*, of Kokkola from 1696 remains. This two-storey building with a high pitched roof and a small clock turret on the ridge is an exceptionally fine representative of its type.

Churches

"The Finnish wooden church is most appealing to posterity as a timber structure, creaky and slightly worn with age, with often puzzling details held together by a relatively precise geometry of proportions which nevertheless lets them speak their own 'dialects'."

LARS PETTERSSON 1989

Of the church architecture of the 17th century in Finland, only sixteen wooden churches, five stone churches and six bell towers have been preserved. The simplest chapels or preaching

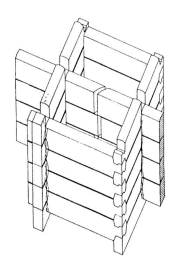

houses did not always differ too much from residential houses; in the largest town and parish churches, however, traditional carpentry skills reached impressive architectural heights. Many wooden churches have burned down, some quite recently. Up to the early twentieth century, many were pulled down without a second thought to make way for larger churches of brick. Some localities preserved their old wooden church near the new stone church as a historical curiosity.

One of the best-preserved is the church of offering at Luoto, Pyhämaa, built from 1647 to 1652 on an island located on the ancient shipping route from Uusikaupunki to Rauma. Corner-timbered with feather joints, the church has a simple basilican plan and a three-sided apse. The low pitched roof is hipped at the east end. The low, dimly lit interior is unique both as a spatial experience and because the walls and ceiling are covered by colourful, primitivistic paintings by Christian Wilbrandt.

When the length of an oblong church exceeds that of an ordinary log, the side walls must be built of at least two consecutive series of timbers. No matter how carefully the timbers were spliced, the roof and its trusses would weigh down so heavily on the walls that without support they would eventually bulge outward. The Ostrobothnian master carpenters solved this problem by inventing an ingenious structure of pillars and tie beams which made it possible to build a church of any length. In the support structure, splices to the wall timbers were placed inside hollowed-out pillars, which were connected on the inside by diagonal and longitudinal supports. The joints between the tie beams and pillars were strengthened with profiled brackets carved from a different piece of timber. Thus the weight of the roof was divided evenly between the tie beams, the top course of the side walls, the pillars and the end walls. A board vault was nailed from below to the bottom of the roof truss. Most churches had two supporting pillars, or block pillars, a few had one, and the longest ones had three. A tower was often placed at the west end, an important landmark for mariners. The vestry was at the chancel end on the north side of the nave, the porch nearer the west end.

The block-pillar system was probably invented in Ostrobothnia back in the fifteenth century. It became common in the seventeenth century, also spreading to Norrland on the other side of the Gulf of Bothnia. Some churches were still built using this system in the eighteenth century. The plan required builders versed in the refined logic of timber structures, and was based on the forms of long, narrow Gothic stone churches. The overall look of the seventeenth-century block-pillar church was Gothic. The oldest church of the kind with a well-documented history was the church of Salo, or Saloinen, which

Tornio Church.

Drawing of Tornio Church and bell tower,
M. Outhier, 1736–37.

Sodankylä Church.

---

burned down in 1930. Pettersson has traced its history back to the 1490s. Armas Lindgren, then a young student of architecture, depicted the interior in 1896 in a charming watercolour. The basic plan of Saloinen Church was followed by the builders of Hailuoto Church (burned down in 1968) about 1620. The oldest church of this type to have been preserved is in Vöyri (built 1626–27), though it was enlarged to a cruciform plan in the late 18th century.

A towerless church with two pairs of support pillars and crowned by a high pitched roof was built in Tervola from 1687 to 1689. The walls are sided with vertical weatherboarding painted red and dating from the 18th century, but the uncovered interior reveals the details of the original structure. The small church of Kempele, built a couple of years later, has only one pair of supporting pillars. The steep pitched roof harmoniously echoes the sharp rise of the slender steeple. The simple interior is embellished by paintings done by Mikael Toppelius in the 1780s.

Tornio town church, consecrated in 1686, is the most richly decorated of the block-pillar churches. The rectangular main room is strengthened by three pairs of support pillars. The west tower has a tall, tapering pinnacle. The unusual ceiling consists of four domical vaults with fine frescoes by Lauri Gallenius. The ornate rood screen, the pulpit and the magnificent window and door frames were carved by Nils Jacobson Fluur in the 18th century. Next to the church is a fine Gothic bell tower, the oldest preserved in Ostrobothnia.

The small northern church of Sodankylä is Finland's best-preserved wooden church. Without weatherboarding or paint, its old timber structures seem movingly authentic in the dimly-lit interior. The homely ornamentation, consisting of a triangular pattern of shingles on the pitched roof, a ridge beam and three poles for weather vanes, accentuates the attractive grey of aged wood. The peace of this backwoods church on the brink of a growing population centre and at a major crossroads was assured when a sturdy timber fence similar to the original one was built around the churchyard in 1980.

The international Renaissance reached Finland in the seventeenth century, bringing with it a new kind of ecclesiastical architecture, the cruciform church. The first churches of this type were built in the 1660s, commissioned by powerful noblemen who wished to emulate the new style which had already made its breakthrough in Stockholm. The new churches were built in

towns, in counties or baronies, or in parishes where the nobility had considerable land holdings, in ironworks communities, or in remote places where it was up to the crown to build churches. The first cruciform churches varied considerably in detail. Pettersson has concluded that the clients who commissioned them acquired plans from Sweden, which the local carpenters then applied individually to their own traditional skills. Thus, the roofs of these simple cruciform churches were built, as a rule, on high, steep trusses in mediaeval fashion. Local builders' variants of the new church type developed only in the following century. In Ostrobothnia, the popularity of the block-pillar church was unshakeable; with its tower functioning as a landmark for seamen, it had proved satisfactory in every way. The first cruciform churches in Ostrobothnia were not built until the 1690s.

The tiny cruciform church commissioned by Arvid Horn for Karuna and built 1685–86 was the first building to be moved to the Seurasaari open-air museum in Helsinki in the 1910s. A popular church for summer weddings, it has adjusted to its new site well enough to provide an excellent example of a 'functional museum piece'. The bell tower, built in Karuna in 1767, was moved to Seurasaari along with the church.

The church of Hiittinen (1685–86) is the oldest cruciform church preserved in southwestern Finland. The ground plan is in the form of a cross with arms of even length, with a pyramid-roofed central tower accentuated by a narrow spire rising from the crossing. The chapel church of Houtskari island, built 1703–04, has a similar ground plan but no central tower. The adjacent bell tower was built some fifty years later.

The simple cruciform church of Elimäki, built 1678, is the best-preserved of its type in eastern Uusimaa despite later additions of horizontal weatherboarding and cement shingle roofing. It was built at the instigation of Fabian Caspersson Wrede, governor of Viipuri province at the time, whose family was the largest landowner in the region. The master builder was Petter Lohman. The Elimäki interior contains an interesting Gothic touch: the nave ceiling consists of five even-crowned domes of equal height with central rings and ribs similar to those in Hollola. The altarpiece and pulpit, older than the building itself, are striking, as are the fragmentary remnants of fresco decoration. The splendid bell tower was built 1795–97 by Aatami Juhonpoika Marttila.

Of the cruciform churches in the Päijänne-Kymenlaakso region, the church of Iitti, built in 1693, has also been preserved to some extent. The most striking exterior feature is the distinct outward bend of the roof at the eaves. Its master builder David Juhananpoika also built the later demolished churches of Asikkala and Hartola.

Solid granite stonework of the Hyve (Virtue) Bastion in the fortress of Suomenlinna.

The eighteenth century

The Great Northern War (1700–21) and the Russian occupation of Finland, known as the Great Wrath, from 1713 to 1721 meant a harsh break between the seventeenth and eighteenth centuries. In the peace of Uusikaupunki in 1721, Sweden ceded the towns of Viipuri, Käkisalmi and Sortavala to Russia. Sorely tried by the war, Finland had only some 320,000 inhabitants when it ended. Reconstruction got promisingly under way, but was interrupted by the war of 1742–43, known as the Lesser Wrath, and more land in the east had to be surrendered. The eastern border was drawn along the river Kymi: the towns of Savonlinna, Lappeenranta, and Hamina were now in Russian territory.

Not until the latter half of the century did the general economic boom in Europe reach Finland. This period, later known as the age of freedom and utility, brought development and prosperity under a mercantilist economic policy and a physiocratic agricultural policy. Tar burning and the sawmill industry produced materials for the countless sailing ships plying the world's oceans.

Advances in the natural sciences put culture in a new perspective. Building techniques improved; the construction of fortifications led to the spread of stoneworking skills; the tiled stove was invented, glass windows became common, and the comfort of living increased. Building came under strict supervision. From 1776 on, the

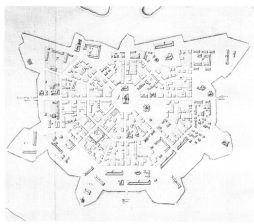

Hamina, town plan and aerial view.

drawings of all public buildings had to be sent to the superintendent of public works in Stockholm for review. Statutes calling for the use of fireproof materials were enacted to improve fire safety and to save forests. In Finland, however, they could be implemented only in exceptional cases. The parishes applied for special dispensations and went on building their churches from the traditional material, wood. Uniformity of architecture was further promoted by model plans, the impact of which reached vernacular architecture through the example of military quarters.

The development of towns speeded up with the abolition of the staple system in 1765, enabling the towns of Ostrobothnia to export their own goods. The bourgeoisie prospered and the crafts developed in accordance with the doctrine of economic liberalism. The rapid progress made in the latter half of the eighteenth century was reflected in rapid population growth. By the end of the era of Swedish rule in 1809, Finland had a population of 900,000, an increase of more than 50 per cent over the 1770s.

The Baroque style dominated Finnish art in the early eighteenth century. The influence of the subsequent Rococo period is even more difficult to show in architecture than in the pictorial arts; it is most clearly visible in the furnishing of country estates. King Gustavus III made a journey to Italy towards the end of the century which aroused his interest in Antiquity; this had an almost immediate impact on Finland. The king's neoclassical dream of a Nordic Pantheon came true when the circular church of Hämeenlinna designed by his court architect Louis-Jean Desprez was completed in 1798.

Fortifications

Finland's trials during the war had revealed the weakness of her defences: planning of new fortifications began in the 1720s. The construction of fortresses in Finland was in fact Sweden's largest public building project during the 18th century. The Russians in turn built fortifications in the lands east of the river Kymi, their main purpose being to protect St. Petersburg, the new capital founded by Peter the Great at the mouth of the river Neva in 1703.

The architecture of this region, Old Finland, shows the stratification of Swedish and Russian aspirations, of two-way defence. Fortification, the art of building fortresses, was a military science; in the eyes of later generations, all credit is due to the officers who planned fortifications, thereby producing imposing architecture. Both the Swedes and Russians applied the general

Commandant's house, Loviisa.

European fortification theory of the period, published in numerous manuals. According to Rainer Knapas, however, Swedish and Russian fortifications had their own idiosyncrasies. The Swedes confined themselves to a restrained Rococo Classicism named after Carl Hårleman. The Russians paid increasing attention to the visual impressiveness of fortress architecture: the Russian Classicism of the late 1780s was quite grand in places. Russian military engineers received a grounding in the Classics, when Vignola, Alberti, Vitruvius, and in part Palladio were translated into Russian.

Sweden's fortification programme was directed in the 1720s by Axel Löwen, who drew up plans for the defence of Helsinki, the modernization of Häme Castle, and the fortification of the east coast, e.g. by building fortresses in Hamina and Lappeenranta. Most of Löwen's plans were curtailed or shelved, but the building of Hamina got under way before the Russians took over there, and Löwen went down in architectural history as the initiator of a unique monument: a circular town. The town plan and fortification plan of Hamina from 1723 shows a town encircled by fortifications, with an octagonal central square in which eight radiating streets terminate; these streets are intersected by ring streets following the form of the square.

Hamina was accorded town rights in 1723, and construction began. The circular town was

an ideal of Renaissance theoreticians, but less than ten of the type were built in all of Europe. The model suited Hamina in that the town was built on virgin soil, and the round town plan could be fitted perfectly to the military works. Hamina burned down in the war of 1742, but the Russians rebuilt it systematically, making only slight alterations to the master plan. Later fires and the indifference of the present century have made serious inroads on the historical town, but the unusual plan still makes it distinctive. Hamina's most significant buildings are the present city museum, built in the 1760s, the fine three-storey town hall from the 1790s, the town church designed by Carl Ludvig Engel, the Orthodox church, possibly designed by L.T.J. Visconti, and the Classicist reserve officers' school, designed by Jacob Ahrenberg and built in the 1890s as a military academy.

The town of Loviisa was founded in 1746 as Sweden's new eastern outpost. Augustin Ehrensvärd drew up a town plan the next year, which according to Henrik Lilius was the first in Finland to be based on purely Classicist principles, the finest town plan of the era. The plan called for an axially symmetrical town protected like its Dutch forerunners by a belt of fortifications. Its backbone was to have been a T-shaped canal, on both sides of which Ehrensvärd grouped a dynamic composition of blocks and plots of varied shape. In addition to a new com-

Painting by Elias Martin depicting the construction of Sveaborg (Suomenlinna).

Augustin Ehrensvärd lies buried in the courtyard of the Susisaari stronghold.

plexity, the plan introduced motifs which later became popular, such as shoreline boulevards and radiating streets. Although construction of Loviisa promptly got under way, eventually only two bastions, one barracks, three military buildings, a handful of burghers' houses, and the Commandant's house (1755, today the town museum) were completed.

The supreme achievement of Swedish fortification, and in many ways Finland's central architectural monument of the eighteenth century, was Suomenlinna (originally Sveaborg), a fortress built on a group of six islands off the coast of Helsinki. Construction began in 1748 under Augustin Ehrensvärd; the most intense construction period lasted until 1791. Olof af Hällström claims that Sveaborg was the largest construction project ever undertaken up to then by the Swedish crown. It was one of the keystones of the Swedish defence; later, from 1808 to 1918, it served as a Russian stronghold under the name of Viapori. As a result of a military alliance between Sweden and France, the French contributed sixty-seven barrels of gold to the building project before 1765. Most of the con-

struction work was done by common soldiers, who spent some 100 days a year on the islands. Work stopped for the winter and the soldiers returned home, most of them to Sweden. The workforce was largest in summer 1751, when 6,750 men were assigned to the project. The workers' living conditions were primitive, but construction proceeded apace; Ehrensvärd organized everything with admirable skill. Procurement of building materials provided considerable employment on the mainland, too: a number of nearby parishes supplied building timber and firewood; lime was quarried in Sipoo; bricks were manufactured in Sörnäinen.

On four of the six islands of Suomenlinna, the fortifications form a closed stronghold; the remaining two have defensive lines open to the sea. Taken as a whole, the islands are a historic milieu of highly distinctive character, visually united by the rugged regularity of high, grass-covered earthworks and angular granite structures. The barracks are in the ascetic Classicist style of Hårleman. Many of the structures were only partially completed or later destroyed. The immediate sense of fragmentariness is hard to explain, but part of the reason may be that when walking about the islands one has difficulty in perceiving the relation of the parts to the whole.

Susisaari was the main stronghold from 1750 on. Its works consist of two closed rings of bastions, one within the other. Between them is the

*Porvoo town hall.
Gotthard Flensborg,
1760-61.*

galley harbour on the north side and the garrison square in the southwest. The most important courtyards between the rings were the Grand Court (Iso Linnanpiha) and the Palmstierna Court.

The Grand Court was the finest monumental square in the whole of Finland at the time, and seemed larger than it really was through the use of the Baroque art of illusionist perspective. The northern termination of the quadrilateral courtyard is still formed by the Commandant's house, to which the inner walls of the bastions and the firing platforms rise somewhat obliquely. Two wing buildings originally stood at the lower end, their combined facades forming a semicircle. Access to the courtyard was from a passage which led between these buildings straight to the central axis at the lower end. The Great Court was ruined by demolition and alterations in the late nineteenth century, but its reconstruction has been discussed. The site was consecrated when the tomb of Augustin Ehrensvärd, designed by Carl August Ehrensvärd and Johan Tobias Sergel with contributions by King Gustavus III himself, was placed in its centre in the 1780s.

On the southeast shore of Kustaanmiekka island is the impressively ceremonial King's Gate, bearing an inscription which states that its first stone was laid in 1748 by King Adolphus Frederick. The elegant structure was designed by no less an architect than Carl Hårleman. Although it had no practical function, it served, according to Lars Pettersson, as the symbolic gate to Finland: whoever passed through was lord of the fortress and of the whole country.

Among the Russian additions to Suomenlinna, the Orthodox church built 1850–54 on Iso Mustasaari in Byzantine style provided the fortress with the most clearly Russian touch. As soon as Finland became independent, the decision was taken to convert the church into a Lutheran place of worship. The winner of the architectural competition for the purpose was Einar Sjöström, whose plan cleverly masked the form of the Orthodox church, reinforcing the Swedish atmosphere of the fortress. A writer compared the starkly handsome church with an officer of the Finnish freedom fighters standing at attention.

Towns

During the Great Northern War, the Russians burned down Finland's coastal towns. Reconstruction got to a slow start, as the building of towns took second place to new fortification projects.

One of the first major public buildings of the period was the new town hall of Turku, built 1735–36 under Samuel Berner, a German-born

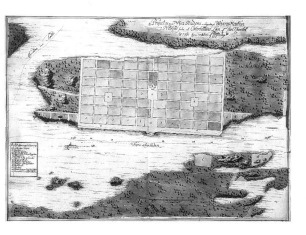

Kaskinen town plan, drawn up by C. J. Cronstedt in 1767 and ratified in 1785.

Aerial view of Kaskinen.

mason and town architect of Turku. It was a two-storey brick structure crowned by an imposing tower at one end of the oblong mediaeval square. The town hall was raised and altered beyond recognition in the 1880s.

The other town halls built in Finland were also two storeys high and had a tower, though not so ostentatious as the one in Turku. Some communities repaired their old seventeenth-century town halls; nevertheless, as Lilius points out, nearly twenty new town halls were built. Other notable public buildings included schools, customs houses and bonded warehouses, and prisons. Most residential buildings were still single-storey wooden houses with a pitched roof. The Quensel House on the river Aura in Turku, today a pharmacy museum, represents a more recent house type with a high hip roof.

The dynamic economic policy of the utilitarian era which followed the 'Lesser Wrath' (the war of 1742–43) sped up the construction of towns. A more varied type of grid plan established itself in town planning. Main streets were built wider than other streets; boulevards and, where possible, shoreline promenades intro-

duced new architectural elements. Private houses as well as town halls were now built in two storeys. The mansard roof became popular in the 1740s. Other than main thoroughfares, streetscapes were high and narrow. Public squares gave the grid plan axial coordination.

A new town, Kaskinen, was founded on the Gulf of Bothnia in 1765. It was planned as the new centre of the west coast, superseding Vaasa and Kristiinankaupunki, which were to be abandoned. Carl Johan Cronstedt's town plan for Kaskinen was ratified in 1785. The rectangular grid, based on four symmetrically placed squares and two main axes, had potential as an elegant framework for large-scale urban development. A semicircular ceremonial wharf was placed on the shoreline boulevard as a terminus to the administrative axis. Lilius cites Kaskinen as a graphic example of the unrealistic approach of over-ambitious town planning. When the plan was drawn up, Kaskinen was a village of two hundred-odd inhabitants; the population barely reached 1500 in the mid-1960s before going into decline again. Nevertheless, when the town's first proper church was built in the 1960s on the site designated by Cronstedt, the original plan was still respected.

Public urban construction – town halls, churches and school buildings – took over the key positions in the townscape. Architecture in general began to attract increasing interest from

Vaasa Court of Appeal, today Mustasaari Church. C. F. Adelcrantz, 1786.

the mid eighteenth century on. The officers and masons employed in fortification were skilled professionals, representatives of a new class. Brickmaking skills became widespread. Stone buildings continued to be favoured officially, now with better chances of success. Lilius notes, however, that stylistic trends were not uniform. A fairly conventional design prevailed in most architecture. Rococo Classicism was the dominant style in stone buildings; yellow was the fashionable colour. In contrast, wooden buildings continued to be painted with the traditional red, though now vertical corner boards were used to imitate the effect of stone.

The finest stone buildings were erected in Porvoo. The town hall, built after the town burned down in 1760, is a two-storey structure with a mansard roof in Hårleman's Classicist style. According to Pekka Kärki, its master builder was Gotthard Flensborg, a fortress builder. The grammar school was built 1758–59 next to the mediaeval church to plans drawn up by Samuel Berner and modernized by Carl Johan Cronstedt, the superintendent of public works. A tower was added to the town hall with a dial as an important new feature; the school also requested a tower to use as an observatory. As a result of Cronstedt's contribution, the Classicism of the grammar school (today used by the cathedral chapter) is more precise than that of the town hall: it clearly expresses the relation-

ship between bearing and borne structures. The tower was never built.

In Helsinki, Samuel Berner built a two-storey business mansion for the merchant Johan Sederholm in 1757, the town's most opulent private house at the time. In its present, slightly altered form, the house at the southeast corner of Senate Square alone stands for the scale of 18th-century Helsinki, which vanished all but completely in the disastrous fire of 1808.

The Gustavian period (1775–1809) carried on the policy of busy urban development based on Classicist planning principles. Gustavus III rearranged the division of Finland into provinces, with Hämeenlinna, Oulu, Heinola, and Kuopio as the new provincial capitals. The founding of Kuopio fulfilled the old goal of providing the eastern farming area with a much-needed centre. Local fire and building ordinances supplemented the supervision of urban development.

Stylistically, Henrik Lilius divides the architecture of the Gustavian period into three phases. The Vaasa Court of Appeal (today Mustasaari Church, 1786), placed at the end of a fine tree-lined avenue, represents French Classicism, which came into fashion in the late 1760s, gradually popularizing the Classical system of columns. The mansard roof, however, still harks back to the previous period of Hårleman. The purest example of Gustavian Neo-Classicism proper is Hämeenlinna Church (1797), designed

Hämeenlinna Church. The original circular church was designed by Louis Jean Desprez (1798), the tower and transepts are later additions.

Turku Academy. Carl Christopher Gjörwell and Charles Bassi, 1801–15. Reliefs in assembly hall by Erik Cainberg, 1816.

The Sederholm Building at the corner of Senate Square. Samuel Berner 1757.

*Mustio Manor,
Karjaa.*

by Louis Jean Desprez. Turku Academy (1802–11), by Carl Christopher Gjörwell, belongs to the second period of Gustavian Classicism, which replaced columned gables with a simple central *avant-corps*.

Tampere, Finland's most pronouncedly industrial town, was founded in 1779 by Gustavus III as a free town by the Tammerkoski rapids: water was to power the industry to be built there. The first town plan reflects the religious liberalism of the Gustavian period. The grid plan set apart four plots along the edges of the central square for different religious denominations, as it was hoped that Calvinist Huguenots and Presbyterian Scots would join Lutherans and Orthodox in building the new town. Tampere's industrial development only really got under way in the 19th century, however.

The Gustavian period built urban housing of great variety. The rectangular, pitched-roof house – in various sizes – was still popular. The wealthy built two-storey houses, usually with a mansard roof. The roofs were later converted into low pitched roofs, however, in line with the new building ordinance of the early nineteenth century, with the result that this typical 18th-century feature disappeared almost entirely from the townscape in Porvoo and elsewhere. An overwhelming majority of town houses were still wooden, though weatherboarding and paint (which became common during the Gustavian period) gave them a more precisely articulated appearance frequently suggesting stone architecture. Whole clusters of bourgeois stone houses were built in Turku, Helsinki and Porvoo; fine individual specimens were erected in Pietarsaari and Kokkola.

The handsome town houses of the Gustavian period had higher rooms, more space and better internal communications as a result of the enlargement of door openings to permit installation of double doors. A good example is the two-storey house built by Johan Solitander in Porvoo in 1792. From the 1760s on, the windows of such upper middle-class houses were taller by half than before, and instead of small panes the windows had six large ones. Pekka Kärki traces the architectural ideals of the bourgeoisie back to the towns of continental Europe, which Stockholm followed closely. An influential source of the new regularity was *Ritningar på Fyratio Wåningshus af Sten och Trettio af Träd...* (Drawings of forty stone and thirty wood houses), a book of model plans by Captain Carl Wijnblad, published 1755–56.

Manor houses and ironworks

The appreciation of rural productivity during the Age of Utility laid the foundation for the heyday of country estates. Country manor archi-

Fagervik Manor: church in foreground, main building and wings in background.

tecture, too, entered a new phase as the officers in charge of the fortification programme and the master masons in the cities grew more skilful. The most influential builder and planner was Christoffer Friedrich Schröder (1722–89), Turku town architect and alderman of the masons' guild, who planned houses for the owners of nearby manors and ironworks. According to Elias Härö, Schröder's architectural ideas were typically cautious for a provincial architect: he had no ambitions as an innovator, preferring to adhere to the safe, established forms of the late Baroque period as recorded in model books. Schröder's work included at least the following two-storey brick manor houses: Fagervik in Inkoo, Lapila in Naantali, Lempisaari in Askainen, Teijo in Perniö and Viksberg in Paimio. He also designed several manor houses built of wood.

Construction of the two-storey wooden manor house of the Mustio ironworks in Karjaa began in 1782 to Schröder's plans. The client, Magnus Linder, was determined to have a grand manor in the latest style, and he sent Schröder's drawings, reminiscent of Wijnblad's pattern books, to an architect in Stockholm who had found favour with the king. Erik Palmstedt had just returned from a study trip to Italy, and was able to translate Schröder's plans to the precise idiom of Palladian Neo-Classicism. Construction went on until the 1790s, and the result was "solid, warm, decorous and well-proportioned

both inside and out", as Linder wrote in his fire insurance application. The palatial manor, placed at the top of a high slope landscaped in the spirit of the new, free English park ideal, has smooth tongue-and-groove board siding resembling a stone wall. Slender pearl-grey pilasters two storeys high give rhythm to the rectangular, yellow-painted building. A console frieze of the same colour runs under the cornice. The mansard roof has a gable-crowned projecting centre. The eight-paned double-glazed windows on the upper floor were once the largest in Finland. The finest touches of Gustavian Classicism are found in the formal interiors of the upstairs suite: the grand hall has blue and grey tinted wallpaper with painted Tuscan columns amid rich Classicist ornament.

One of Schröder's most extensive planning assignments was the renovation of the Fagervik ironworks buildings. Johan Wilhelm Hising and Mikael Hising bought up the ruined works, repairing and modernizing the industrial facilities and housing. Under Schröder's direction, the workshops were built of grey granite, the workers' housing along the mill thoroughfare of wood, and the modern tinning plant of brick. All the main production buildings had a mansard roof. The wing of the residence on the lake side of the courtyard was built first, the main building in 1773. A plastered timber wing building completed the formal courtyard. The manor house

Pihlajavesi Church.
Matti Åkerblom,
1780-82.

towers above a large complex of production buildings, which even includes a separate church.

The two-storey, mansard-roofed main building of Fagervik is pure Rococo Classicism. The interiors include charming Rococo tapestries with botanical ornament, temple ruins and Chinese motifs painted in bright colours.

A formal French-style garden was laid out in front of the manor house; the slopes were terraced. An English-style park of some 100 acres was cleared and planted behind the manor. The only Chinese pavilion in Finland was erected on a lakeside in the park in the 1780s.

The humbler country estates produced the forms of Rococo Classicism with traditional timber construction methods. An attractive example is Pukkila Manor, built in the 1760s in Piikkiö and today a museum. The room arrangement derives from Wijnblad; the fixed furnishings have Rococo touches. The Rococo interior of Jakkarila Manor in Porvoo is on display at the National Museum: the dining room, with its fine pictorial tapestries, occupies an entire room of the museum.

Wooden churches

In the eighteenth century, the growing population and denser settlement needed new church-es. Only some fifteen new parishes proper were established in Finland during the whole century: instead, old parishes set up over 120 dependent 'chapel districts'. This meant busy construction activity towards the end of the century: a total of 11 stone churches and 120 wooden churches, and a further 130 bell towers, were built.

The master builders were men of the people, who learned their skills from their elders, often their fathers. The best-known builders include Antti Piimänen and his son Mikael from the southwest and Matti Åkerblom and his nephew Matti Åkergren from Häme. Antti Hakola and his son Gabriel were from southern Ostrobothnia; Matti Honka and Antti, Matti and Kaapo Hakola from central Ostrobothnia, Simo Silvén – whose father and son were also church builders – from northern Ostrobothnia. Juhana and Matti Salonen worked in eastern Finland and Karelia. The most renowned of all, however, was another Ostrobothnian, Jaakko Tuomaanpoika Rijf (1753–1808), whose father Tuomas Kaarlenpoika Rijf was a mason and carpenter. Jaakko Rijf was the first local master to receive academic architectural instruction in Stockholm. The career of his son Kaarle Jaakonpoika Rijf (1783–1808) was lamentably brief, as he and his father died in a fever epidemic in Stockholm during construction of the Kungsholm church tower.

The local master builders were not familiar

*Petäjävesi Church.
Jaakko Leppänen,
1763–65; bell tower
by Erkki Leppänen,
1821.*

with the principal monuments of the European Baroque, and yet the various cruciform churches they produced can be seen as reduced versions of the Baroque idiom, a complex strand in the European history of the central-plan church. The styles of the great world reached the northern periphery through many intermediate stages. Wood architecture interestingly combined old traditions with new influences from east and west. The closest model, of course, was Stockholm, especially the Church of St. Catherine designed by Jean de la Vallée, a large cruciform church under construction from 1656 to the 1690s.

Between 1765 and 1807, over a hundred church and belfry designs were sent to the Office of the Royal Superintendent for statutory approval. The Office usually responded by sending the congregation its own, more up-to-date proposal for the design of a church of requisite size; the local masters in turn provided their own interpretation of this plan. The final result was often closer to the local designer's original ideas than the officially approved plans. Lars Pettersson has investigated the procedure in detail; the following account should be taken as a free summary of his extensive research.

Simple cruciform churches continued to be built in southwestern Finland throughout the 18th century. Antti Piimänen built Dragsfjärd Church in 1755 to an even-armed cross plan with

a small central tower with a square base rising from the ridge crossing of the pitched roof. The original ceiling consisted of two barrel vaults with an octagonal board dome at the crossing. Cupolas of this type became common in Finnish churches in the mid eighteenth century; the one in Dragsfjärd was among the first.

The oblong type with a bell tower at the west end continued to be favoured in southwestern Finland. Antti Piimänen (1714–1775) was the leading proponent of this type with his churches in Marttila (1765) and Längelmäki (1772). The drawings for Marttila Church are the oldest known plans for a wooden church in Finland sent to Sweden for approval. The Superintendent's Office rejected the drawings, but the parish went ahead anyway and quickly erected the church with an onion-dome tower according to Piimänen's original plan.

The churches of Kuorevesi (1779), Kuru (1781) and Pihlajavesi (1780–82) were built to the hall plan with west tower by Matti Åkerblom (1740–1819), an apprentice of Antti Piimänen, who introduced this church type in the Häme heartland. The harmonious church of Kuru boasts a tall, handsome west tower with a bulging, turnip-shaped intermediate level between the typical onion dome and the bell chamber.

The ten holdings and four tenant farms of the remote village of Pihlajavesi joined forces to build a wooden church which still radiates a

Keuruu Church. Antti Hakola 1759.

Cruciform church plans, after Lars Pettersson: top left, even-armed cross; centre, double cruciform plan; right, cruciform plan with inner corners bevelled; bottom left, cruciform plan with outer corners bevelled; right, 24-cornered cruciform plan.

Kuortane's 24-cornered church. Antti Hakola 1777.

Ylihärmä Church. Kaapo Hakola 1787.

---

sense of peace. The traveller must take a long, winding road through the forest to reach the church: the seemingly remote location was chosen because it was approximately equidistant from the various builders' homes. A belfry with an onion dome rises from the west end of the building; the walls are joined with locked short joints and unboarded; the tarred timbers shine in the light which seeps through the branches of tall spruce trees. Inside, the even strokes of the broadaxe have left their mark on the unpainted walls.

The Ostrobothnian masters first started building simple cruciform churches in the 18th century; by the end of that century they had developed ingenious variations of the type, culminating in the church with twenty-four corners.

One of the simple early designs was the church built at Paltaniemi, Paltamo by master builder Johan Knubb from Vöyri. The main attraction of the church, apart from its lovely site, is the interior. The whitewashed walls display Rococo frescoes (1778–81) by Emanuel Granberg.

The visitor to Lapland can find a small church with an almost even-armed cruciform plan near the shore of Lake Iso Pielpajärvi in Inari. The church was built 1754–60; the ground floor of the somewhat younger bell tower next to the west gable is used as an anteroom.

Petäjävesi Church, built 1763–65 by Jaakko Leppänen of Vesanka, has won deserved acclaim in recent years as an atmospheric venue for summer concerts. Together with the adjoining bell tower, built in 1821 in Ostrobothnian style, this cruciform church with a high roof stands out as one of the most beautiful and best-preserved ensembles of Finnish wood architecture. To quote Pettersson's description: "Bare, unpainted wood predominates both the exterior and the interior; only the doors, the beams, level with the lower end of the vaults, and the wooden vault ribs have painted red ochre decoration. The timber surfaces of the interior display a silky, greyish patina, whereas the vaults glow in all the hues of red pine. The atmosphere of the interior is inimitable. Concentrated, logical architectural forms, the soft contours of wall timbers and vault boarding, and the soft light entering from the windows combine to produce an effect of intimacy accentuated by the slightly

irregular floor beams and sturdy pews with pan-elled and gently profiled ends."

Antti Antinpoika Hakola (1709–1778) was one of the most renowned church builders of central Ostrobothnia. Among his finest still ex-tant works are the churches of Keuruu and Vir-rat. Since the 1890s, Keuruu Church (1756–69) has been merely a tourist attraction in the centre of the village, overshadowed by the new brick church. The rhomboid pattern of its high shingle roof and the boldly soaring belfry are well worth seeing. Here Hakola produced a variant of the oblong church with west tower; the interior ap-proaches a cruciform plan. The ceiling is a barrel vault and the walls are strengthened with tie beams under the eaves. The white painted inte-rior was decorated in the 1780s with frescoes in Rococo style. The octagonal vestry behind the church was added to the east transept in 1832, when the windows were enlarged.

The wish to enlarge and focus the interior of the cruciform church led to the bevelling of cor-ners in the transepts and crossing. The division of walls into shorter components enabled build-ers to use shorter timbers, making it easier to find suitable trees and promoting the preserva-tion of forests. The most influential architectural forerunners were Stockholm's Riddarholm Church and the Churches of Adolphus Freder-ick in Karlskrona and Stockholm; the ultimate source consisted of the plans of Bramante and

his successors for St. Peter's in Rome. By the time the plan with internal bevelling became popular, external bevelling was on the way out after being fashionable for a quarter of a centu-ry. The 24-cornered cruciform church was a brief experiment during the period when the two styles overlapped.

Kiiminki Church, built by Matti Honka in 1760, has preserved its original interior. The church has twenty corners, and the gently pitched shingle roof follows the ground plan. A tall vane pole with a weathercock rises from the ridge crossing. The interior has barrel vaulting; the white painted walls still have the original timbering and delightful frescoes by Mikael Toppelius. The adjacent bell tower was built in 'Bothnian Renaissance' style in 1777.

Virrat has a cruciform church basically similar to Kiiminki. It was built 1773–74 by Antti Hakola, who completed his work two years later by erecting a bell tower in front of the church. The vestry, an extension of the chancel, dates from 1859.

Antti Hakola was the first master builder to build a church with twenty-four corners, bevel-led both inside and out. The red painted church of Kuortane, built 1777, is covered by a high patterned shingle roof echoing the plan form. A large, onion-domed ridge turret rises from the ridge crossing. The overall harmony is broken only by the ornamental frames of the later en-

Double cruciform church of Lappee. Juhana Salonen, 1794.

larged windows. The walls lean outward as they rise, emphasizing the sculpturesque solidity of form. The original interiors emphasized centrality. The altar was placed at the southeast bevel; later the congregation moved it to the usual position at the head of the east transept.

Antti Hakola's son Kaapo built a 24-cornered church in Ylihärmä (1785–87) with the walls of the transept even more inclined than at Kuortane; Ylihärmä Church still bears a strong resemblance to the original plan for Kuortane Church.

The parishioners of Ruovesi realized at the end of the 18th century that their old church, built during the previous century, had grown small. After a vote between a hall plan and a cruciform plan, the congregation commissioned Matti Åkerblom to build a cruciform church. The 24-cornered church with a high hip roof was consecrated in 1778. The vaulting is sculpturesque: the transept has barrel vaulting and the central area is covered by a high, octagonal, even-crowned ceiling dome. The separate onion-domed bell tower was built by Antti Piimänen in 1772.

The trend towards bigger cruciform churches in eastern Finland followed an independent course of development. The 'double cruciform' plan won particular favour. This type is based on a cross with arms of even length, but the central space is enlarged by extending the inner corners of the cross. The prototypes were two churches in Hamina, the Church of Ulrika Eleonora, which was built 1730–31 and burned down in 1742, and the Church of Elisabeth, built 1748–51 on the same site and destroyed by fire in 1821.

The distinctive outward-narrowing transepts of the Hamina churches were probably dictated by the circular town plan. Henrik Schultz, the builder of the Church of Ulrika Eleonora, passed on the plan to the local master Arvi Junkkarinen, who directed construction of the later Church of Elisabeth. Junkkarinen's main apprentices were August Sorsa and Juhana Salonen. These masters, well versed in traditional corner-jointing techniques, adapted the innovations to the old wooden church tradition, developing them in the process. For a long time, the wooden churches of Savo and Karelia had a richness of detail unknown in the west, with mediaeval and Byzantine touches such as trefoil portals and horseshoe-arched doors. The trefoil portal carved by Arvi Junkkarinen for Kärkölä Church in 1754, however, is known only from a drawing made by Selim A. Lindqvist in 1892.

The Church of Lemi northwest of Lappeenranta contains unique, beautifully renovated trefoil vaulting. This cruciform church was built 1786 by Juhana Salonen (1738-early 1800s). The transepts narrow outwards and the shingles of the steep roof form a rhomboid pattern. An

*Vimpeli Church.
Jaakko Tuomaan-
poika Rijf, 1807.*

octagonal lantern soars above the crossing. The board vaulting with a trefoil-shaped cross section dominates the spacious interior; the cap of the dome, which repeats this motif, is its crowning glory. The adjacent bell tower was rebuilt in the 1930s to the original 1821 plans of Juhana Salonen's son Matti (1761–1823). Matti Salonen directed construction of the double cruciform churches of Uusikirkko, Venjoki and Kivennapa, all in territory ceded to the Soviet Union after World War II.

The first Finnish church with a double cruciform plan after Hamina's Church of Elisabeth was built 1754 in Mikkeli by August Sorsa; it burned down in 1806. Larger than the Hamina church, Mikkeli Church had corner extensions, a central tower and a vast pyramid roof. The other early churches of this type are also known only from historical documents. Lappee Church, built by Juhana Salonen and consecrated in 1794, is the only double cruciform church to have survived: it stands today in the centre of the modern town of Lappeenranta. The arms of the cross narrow outward, but the corner extensions between them are rectangular. The vestry and anterooms are at the transept ends. The large, complex volume is capped by a pyramid roof. The vaulting is unusually bold.

The work of Jaakko Rijf in the late 18th century occupies an interesting position at the intersection between local building and later academic architecture. After his academic studies, he favoured an even-armed cross with internal bevelling as his basic plan. He placed the vestry at the end of the east transept and the altar usually in the bevel between the east and south arms of the cross; he used pilasters and entablatures to enliven the interiors. His churches had low barrel vaults for the transepts and a board dome formed by pendentives and a largish cap. The size of the central tower depended on the size and number of bells. Rijf used pilaster strips, pilasters or columns for the external walls. The finest example of the latter type is the church of Oravainen, built in 1797.

Vimpeli Church was Jaakko Rijf's crowning achievement. The dodecagonal ground plan is covered by a large, polygonal dome. The angular ceiling follows the forms of the roof. The centralizing tendency of the times culminated in 1807 in Vimpeli Church, which imitates the central plan of Rome's Pantheon as closely as is possible with the corner-timbering technique. Jaakko Rijf's immediate model was, of course, Hämeenlinna Church, designed by Louis Jean Desprez and completed in 1798.

Helsinki's Senate Square. Foreground: University, Nicholas Church and Senate.

The nineteenth century

The transfer of power

Finland was annexed by the Russian Empire in 1809, and became an autonomous Grand Duchy ruled by Czar Alexander I. The historian Matti Klinge has pointed out that Sweden ceded a mere conglomeration of provinces to Russia, but the Porvoo Diet united them as a state "raised to the rank of nations". Finland's various regions and tribes began to grow together, no longer with and through Stockholm but with each other, on terms dictated from the new capital, Helsinki.

The Finnish Intendant's Office was established in Turku in 1810. It was charged with maintaining all government buildings and with planning and supervising all public building projects. Although to begin with the new Office only had a staff of two, it provided the first official employment for trained architects in Finland, as Jarkko Sinisalo points out.

The first director of the Intendant's Office was Charles (Carlo) Bassi (1772–1840), an Italian trained in Stockholm, who had been working in Turku from 1802, supervising the completion of the Academy Building designed by C.G. Gjörwell. One of his finest independent works is the Trapp House near the Academy, the main building of the present-day Åbo Akademi, Turku's Swedish-language university. Though he was soon overshadowed by his successor Carl

Pohjois-Esplanadi row. Right: President's Palace (formerly the Heidenstrauch mansion).

Ludvig Engel, Bassi's contribution to the building of Finland should not be dismissed lightly. Plans carried out under his leadership from 1810 to 1824 included forty-three new churches and church renovations, hospitals, schools, prisons, granaries, bridges and much more. Many further plans were never carried out.

The Gustavian small town of Helsinki was destroyed in November 1808 by a fire in which one third of the 4,000 inhabitants lost their homes. A reconstruction committee set up in 1810 charged Lieutenant Anders Kocke with drawing up a new town plan. Kocke's plan was ratified in 1811.

Construction did not really get under way until 1812, however, when the Czar radically altered the nature of the project by declaring Helsinki the capital of Finland. On the same day, he appointed the military engineer Johan Albrekt Ehrenström, a former courtier of Gustavus III, head of the reconstruction committee. Ehrenström gave short shrift to Kocke's modest grid plan and decisively set about to provide a monumental framework for the new city's growth.

Ehrenström's work progressed gradually, and the final plan was ratified in 1817. Its monumental centre was Senaatintori (Senate Square), an enlarged version of the old Suurtori, or Great Square. The street at the south end of the old square, Suurkatu, was renamed Aleksanterin-katu. Aleksanterinkatu and the other main thoroughfares – the present-day Liisankatu, Unioninkatu and Mariankatu – were laid out wider than the other streets. Unioninkatu was the principal north-south axis leading to the square. Ehrenström laid out the Esplanadi park (bordered by the twin streets Pohjoisesplanadi and Eteläesplanadi) to separate the old town from its new southern extension. He laid out Bulevardi as the main street between Esplanadi and Hietalahti bay; a new suburb sprang up in the present Kamppi district. Houses in the centre had to be built of stone; wood was permitted only in the suburbs. A more uniform block network was achieved by reclaiming Kluuvi Bay. The plan emphasized Helsinki's maritime character, with straight seaside promenades and squares laid out along the shores.

Although the town north of Esplanadi was to be built entirely of stone, concessions had to be made from the principle. Only the wealthiest merchants of Helsinki could afford to build stone houses with two to three storeys along Pohjoisesplanadi to plans by the Swedish-born fortification officer Pehr Granstedt (1764–1828).

Ehrenström's town plan made Senate Square the symbolic heart of the Grand Duchy of Finland, where all the main institutions had an exact place dictated by their function in the hierarchy. He reserved the rocky ledge towering above the northern edge of the square for the

Eckerö customs house and post office, Åland. C.L. Engel, 1828.

Lutheran Church, the east side for the Senate, and the west side for its intended twin, the Governor-General's palace. The old burghers' houses along the south edge were allowed to remain, awaiting modernization. The Imperial Palace, which Ehrenström originally thought of as the square's dominant feature, was placed somewhat offside in the plan, approximately at the present location of the House of Nobility. In the hierarchy of classical architectural theory, the highest position belonged to the Church. Henrik Lilius has traced the roots of Senate Square's architecture via Gustavus Adolphus Square in Stockholm back to Rome's Campidoglio.

Ehrenström's plan provided a solid outline for the construction of a brave new imperial city. All that was missing was an architect skilful enough to design all the monumental buildings required.

Carl Ludvig Engel and Helsinki

Carl Ludvig Engel (1778–1840) received his architect's diploma from the Berlin Bauakademie in 1804. As there was no work in Prussia during the Napoleonic Wars, Engel applied for and received an appointment as city architect of Tallinn. From there he visited Finland for the first time, and caused such a stir in Turku that he

was asked to design an observatory for the Academy even though Bassi had already drawn up plans for it. The Czar approved Engel's plans over Bassi's. This was the first indication that a young architect of real promise had arrived. Today the observatory on Vartiovuori hill is a seafaring museum. Engel spent the years 1813–1816 in St. Petersburg, acquainting himself with the architecture of Giacomo Quarenghi, A.D. Zaharov and C.I. Rossi and familiarizing himself with architectonic innovations.

Ehrenström first met Engel in 1814 and was convinced that he had found his man. Engel had been planning to return to Berlin, but he was appointed architect of the reconstruction committee in 1816, and stayed in Finland for the rest of his life. "Few architects have the good fortune to plan an entire city", as Engel explained his decision in a letter to a friend.

The circumstances for the construction of Helsinki were exceptional in every way. The Czar took a personal interest in architecture, was familiar with the ins and outs of the Neo-Classical style, and meddled with the details of Engel's work, though he was basically pleased with it. He directed the building of a 'Hellas of the North' in order to flaunt the high level of Russian civilization to Europe.

This attitude was reflected in the Åland Islands customs house and post office, built in 1828 on the western cliffs of the island of Eck-

erö, a kind of west facade to Senate Square. The monumental group of stone buildings was much too grand for any practical purpose. The bombastic plan is explained by the fact that Eckerö was the westernmost border outpost of the Imperial Post Office. The buildings stand as a message to all comers that the Czar's Russia was a prosperous and modern country. Alexander I understood the uses of a message carved in stone. There were to be no half-measures in building this new capital and its institutions!

Engel rapidly started work on the buildings for Senate Square. He started by converting the old Bock House at the south end into the Governor-General's residence. The building is known today as the Old Town Hall. The first new building on the square was the Main Guard, in front of the designated church site; its sturdy Doric portico had to make way some twenty years later for the church steps.

The main wing of the Senate overlooking the square was completed in 1822, the south wing in 1824 and the east wing between 1826 and 1828. The north wing was not built at the time. The principal section of the palace of government was articulated according to Quarenghi's Palladian model: a central avant-corps, accentuated by a dome and accompanied by lighter flanking projections, dominates the harmonious three-storey structure. The ponderous composition of the ground floor and the use of the Corinthian

order for columns and porticos refers to the Roman origin of the institution of the Senate. The finest interiors are the stair hall and the throne room on the first floor behind the central portico. According to Kalevi Pöykkö, Engel was particularly proud of his technical feat in vaulting the staircase without any iron supports.

After the fire of Turku, the Czar decided to move the university to Helsinki and designated a plot on the west side of the square for it. The Imperial Alexander University was completed in 1832 as the Senate's twin, a haven of civilization as a counterpart to the administrative palace. Engel used the Ionic order for the main building, designing it as a Temple of Apollo. The general form echoes that of the Senate but the details speak a language of their own. The most monumental spatial sequence in the University consists of a stair hall three storeys high leading up to the semicircular assembly hall. A 20th-century extension altered the character of the assembly hall, but the vestibule, shaped like a Roman atrium, has been restored to its original form quite successfully despite devastation caused by bombs during the last war. When the University was enlarged in the 1930s to occupy a whole city block, J.S. Sirén designed the extension following Engel's style so closely that many forget today that Engel was only responsible for the rectangular wing on the Unionkatu side.

As architect of Helsinki University, Engel

Helsinki University Library. C. L. Engel, 1844.

Viurila Manor stables, Halikko. C. L. Engel, 1840–41.

created a unique academic milieu in the heart of the capital, a sequence of prominent buildings which give the university a more central position in Helsinki's town plan than perhaps in any other capital city. Its southernmost monument is the Observatory, built on Tähtitorninmäki hill in 1834 using the most sophisticated technology available at the time. At the time the hill was completely bare, an ideal place for astronomical observations. Tapio Markkanen notes that Engel was first in the world to use rotatable observatory towers as architectural highlights.

At the corner of Unioninkatu and Liisankatu at the north end of the monumental centre, Engel designed the Clinical Institute, or 'Old Clinic', which opened in 1833. For its clinic for internal medicine, the University later also acquired the Cantonist School for orphan boys, designed by Engel and built 1820–23. Its long, low facade is dominated by a sturdy central portico with Ionic columns. The block is to be turned over to the university within the next few decades, when its attractive courtyards will provide the university with a sheltered campus.

The University Library next to the main building was completed in 1844, after Engel's death. The harmonious facade, with its dominat-

ing Corinthian pilasters and columns, has often been praised as Engel's most beautiful; the spacious, barrel-vaulted halls are their match. The library occupies a prominent site at the corner of Senate Square, where it provides a backdrop to the Cathedral and also fitted in with the long, low portico of the Main Guard, which originally stood in front of the church. Lars Pettersson traced the themes of the interior back to the Thermae of Diocletian in Rome, known to Engel from the French edition of Palladio's scale drawings.

Engel worked on the drawings for the main Lutheran church of Helsinki, known formerly as the Church of Nicholas and today as the Great Church or Cathedral, from 1818 until his death. The wooden 'Old Church', originally intended as a temporary sanctuary for the town's Lutherans until the Nicholas Church was completed, was built 1824–26 outside the old centre. The Orthodox Church of the Holy Trinity was erected in the same years behind the Cathedral.

The planning and building of the Church of Nicholas was fraught with complications. In 1819 Engel wrote to a friend in Berlin that he hoped soon to start building a church with a high central dome, a floor plan in the shape of a Latin cross, and six Corinthian columns on each side. Over the decades, he pared down this typically Neo-Classical design, based on Renaissance theory and practice, to the bare essentials. The un-

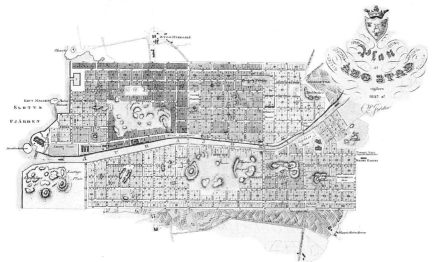

adulterated harmony of proportions Engel envisaged was not, however, allowed to govern the
church entirely. A steep flight of steps replaced
the Main Guard, evidently at the Czar's wish,
and after Engel's death, his successor Ernst
Bernhard Lohrmann placed towers at the corners of the nave crossing. The visitor still finds
Engel's refined geometry in the interior. The
church was finally consecrated in 1852.

Engel's Neo-Classicism is still one of the
chief constituents of Helsinki's architectural
character. He designed a total of some thirty
public buildings in Helsinki, and though ten or
so have been demolished, his main works are
still in uses worthy of their dignity. The Ministry
for Foreign Affairs took over the Naval Barracks (1820) in Katajanokka district in the 1980s,
building the east wing (designed by Engel but
not built) and making other additions. The
Guard Barracks (1822) loom above Kasarmintori (Barracks Square), exuding military severi-
ty. The Seurahuone clubhouse (1833), which
dominates Kauppatori (Market Square), has
been refurbished several times over, and has
served for several decades as City Hall. The
nearby President's Palace is used by the head of
the Finnish state, basically in the form that Engel gave it. He revised the plans for the old
Heidenstrauch merchant's mansion in keeping
with the dignity of the site; later he and his son
Carl Alexander Engel redesigned it as an impe-

rial residence. The Sundman House at Eteläranta is still known as the Victor Ek House after the
forwarding company that used to occupy it,
though the house has changed hands again. The
town palace built 1821 on Etelä-Esplanadi for
the commander of the local division, and taken
over by the Governor-General, who moved
there in 1840, is still often seen on the TV news,
as it is used for Council of State receptions.

Outside the monumental centre, Engel designed numerous residential houses of stone and
wood, which have given way to later, larger
buildings. The block structure, scale and lifestyle
in suburban Helsinki at the time are best studied
in the paintings and drawings of Magnus von
Wright exhibited at the Helsinki City Museum.

From 1824 on, Engel's brief covered the
whole of Finland: as head of the Intendant's
Office, he was responsible for all planning and
public construction in the country. Little by little, he gathered a band of pupils to assist him
and trained them into his staff. Throughout Engel's amazingly prolific career, however, the
number of competent architects in Finland
could be counted on the fingers of one hand.

The Empire-style wooden town

Many towns were ravaged by fire in the early
years of Finland's autonomy under Russian rule,

Turku Orthodox Church. C. L. Engel, 1846.

but reconstruction did not always proceed at the feverish pace of the capital. To begin with, the Intendant's Office did not draw up town plans: it merely supervised the work of surveyors. Town planning continued basically in Gustavian style until the fire of Turku in 1827. Henrik Lilius describes the early years of autonomy as a period of slow, steady growth. One new provincial capital, Mikkeli, was established following a new division of provinces. As a result of an economic policy favouring agriculture, two new inland towns were founded: Jyväskylä and Joensuu.

The towns grew substantially during the first half of the 19th century: their total population, some 50,000 at the beginning of the autonomy years, more than doubled by 1850. Even then, there were only two towns of more than 10,000 inhabitants, Turku and Helsinki.

The fire of Turku in September 1827 was the most devastating ever witnessed in Scandinavia. More than two thirds of the residential parts of the town – a total of 2543 structures, one-tenth of them stone buildings – were destroyed. The Governor-General ordered Engel himself to draw up a new town plan aimed at preventing the spread of fire in the future. Henrik Lilius has investigated the sources and impact of Engel's plan in detail. Completed in 1828, it set the standard for later plans. Although many town plans were still drawn up by local surveyors, the plans were revised by the Intendant's Office to conform to the basic layout of the Turku plan. The surveyors themselves soon adopted the new planning principles.

The key elements of Engel's grid plan were wide streets for the whole town and even wider main streets, in part lined with trees; larger plots; and the stipulation that the plots should be planted to form a green belt of courtyards to prevent the spread of fire. Buildings along the main streets and squares were to be built exclusively of stone. Two-storey wooden houses and mansard roofs were strictly prohibited. Squares were given a commanding position in the low, spacious urban structure. A large park was laid out around Turku Cathedral, and the present Market Square was developed as a new main square and lined with administrative buildings. The town's rocky outcrops were left in their natural state.

To avoid the threat of monotony resulting from the loose plan, Engel held that the rules of architecture could be applied to provide variety in the design of buildings, fences and gates. He drew a number of model block plans to illustrate the new methods. Only isolated fragments of the Empire-style Turku that sprang up in line with these plans have remained, dotted among massive blocks of flats built in later times. The only work of Engel to remain in the Market Square – apart from the outline of the square itself – is the Orthodox church, surrounded by trees, and the

Streetscape in 'new' Porvoo, houses designed by master builder Gustaf Westerberg in 1848.

Turku Swedish Theatre (1836–38), squashed between commercial buildings. Engel's contribution to the latter consisted of corrections to elevations drawn by the self-taught town architect Per Gylich. The Orthodox Church of St. Alexandra was built 1839–46 by imperial decree on a plot reserved in the original plan for the town hall. It has a circular plan with evenly spaced Corinthian columns surrounding the interior. Outside, Doric temple gables projecting in four directions bring to the compact plan a subtle reference to cruciform churches.

Porvoo got a new Empire-style town plan drawn up by Engel in 1832 for a rather unusual reason. Passing through on his travels, Czar Nicholas I had noticed that the old town fell far short of current standards, and suggested that a new town plan was needed. From our perspective today, it was a mercy that old Porvoo was almost entirely spared from the new order: only the part south of the main street, the present Mannerheiminkatu, was built to Engel's plan. A large, coherent town district was built along the river Porvoo; this area in turn has been threatened with demolition since the 1960s.

The verdant, spacious layout is at its best in the vicinity of the museum home of the poet Johan Ludvig Runeberg. Single-storey houses with horizontal weatherboarding and light Classicist accents stand on sturdy stone foundations. Board fences echo the horizontal course of the

facades, hiding the fertile gardens from the eyes of passers-by. Only the top branches of deciduous trees reach out over the fences to the street. The only entrance to the courtyard is through a lockable gate; the only entrance to the house is from the courtyard. There was enough variety in the handiwork of the local master builders to avoid a sense of monotony.

Hämeenlinna needed a new town plan after a disastrous fire in 1831. Engel's plan was ratified the next year and construction soon followed. Up to the 1960s, Hämeenlinna was one of Finland's most uniform Empire towns: now one must hunt among the apartment blocks near 'Pikkutori', or Small Square, for the last vestiges of the period. The seat of the provincial government, built 1836 at the north end of the square, has been restored as a representative example of Engel's work. The ground floor originally housed the provincial tax office and chancery; the governor's residence was upstairs.

For the town plan of the new provincial capital of Mikkeli, Engel combined his own type plan with a group of public buildings previously suggested by the engineer F.F. Gyldén. The composition of Kirkkopuisto Park, the market square, and the axis of shops between them has been preserved from the 1838 plan. The park, however, only contains a bandstand, and the sheer weight of the huge prefabricated apartment blocks surrounding it appears to crush En-

Pori Town Hall.
C. L. Engel 1841.

gel's well-proportioned hospital building at the corner of the market square. A new wing has been added to the Provincial Government building (1843), designed by Engel to occupy the west side of the market square, and the town hall he had envisaged on the south side was not built until the present century, when the line of shops also received their present form. And yet despite all this, the centre of Mikkeli has a distinctively urban character that is largely due to its original town plan and oldest buildings.

The grandest town hall of Engel's period was built 1839–41 in Pori, on a commanding site at the north end of the main square. It has two storeys and a hipped roof, with Doric pilasters running the full height of the central projection. The building's height is further emphasized by a fine clock tower, built at the townspeople's wish partly as a fire lookout.

Urban architecture diversified during the early years of Finnish autonomy, as Henrik Lilius has pointed out in many works. The architecture of town halls, schools, hospitals, buildings for poor relief, hospitals, fire stations, warehouses and new building types such as clubhouses and shop buildings developed between the conflicting pressures of practical needs and stylistic aspiration for a uniform Classicist idiom. Building legislation developed: the general building ordinance for towns, under preparation since the 1810s, was ratified in 1856.

Church architecture under Bassi and Engel

The Finnish Intendant's Office inherited the work of its Swedish predecessor in church building as in other architecture: it inspected and revised plans sent in by parishes and drew up plans of its own. Ville Lukkarinen has studied the scope of this work. Some 180 new churches were built in Finland between 1810 and 1865. Of these, 43 were built during Bassi's period, 44 under Engel, and 72 during the term (1841–65) of Engel's successor Ernst Bernhard Lohrmann; another 21 churches were built without the Office's involvement. The tug-of-war between local masters and official good taste gradually died down. Stone churches were still rare exceptions. Almost all rural parishes applied for and received Senate permission to build their church of wood.

The cruciform plan remained popular. Only two hall churches, in Somerniemi (1812–13) and Lapinlahti (1822–26), were built during Charles Bassi's term of office.

Under Bassi, the Intendant's Office devised several variations of the vernacular double cruciform plan. Some of these, such as the churches of Ylitornio (1811) and Mikkeli (1812), had projections at the corners reaching as high as the transepts and a pyramid roof above the central square rising higher than their pitched roofs. In

'Old Church' of
Tampere. Charles
Bassi, 1824;
bell tower by
C. L. Engel, 1829.

others, such as the churches of Parikkala (1812) and Savitaipale (1821), the projections were lower than the main body of the building.

Among the finest and best-preserved of the churches designed by Bassi is Tampere's 'Old Church'. It was completed 1824 on one of the four plots along Keskustori (the central square) reserved for different religious denominations in the town plan of 1780. Stylistically, the restrained churches of the Bassi period still represent Gustavian Classicism.

Under Engel, the clear tectonics and consistent use of richer decoration of the German-St. Petersburg Empire school prevailed in church architecture and other building. Ville Lukkarinen has traced back the origin of these plans to German publications, including the published plans of Karl Friedrich Schinkel.

The parishes' own planning initiatives petered off: most parishes were content to order their church, merely specifying its size and desired plan type – cruciform, double cruciform, or longitudinal with a west tower. The Office developed model plans which were carried out in various sizes and with variation in the use of Classicist ornament. The cruciform plan remained popular: of the 51 preserved church plans from Engel's period (44 were built), only thirteen were hall churches.

Ville Lukkarinen has summed up the main 'Engelian' church type as follows: "The most

characteristic religious architecture of the Empire period is represented by a group of cruciform churches with internally bevelled corners and an octagonal or round dome with lantern, resting on a high, octagonal attic and rising above the central crossing. The interior has a somewhat smaller domical ceiling. Nine such churches were built between 1826 and 1849: Alajärvi, Lapua, Isojoki, Pyhäjoki, Heinävesi, Saarijärvi, Luumäki, Veteli and Kymi."

The earliest church in this group was that of Alajärvi. Its first plan was drawn up in 1823 by Heikki Kuorikoski, an Ostrobothnian master builder. Assisted by Anton Wilhelm Arppe, the first 'conductor', or construction engineer, at the Intendant's Office, Engel modernized Kuorikoski's plan. They replaced the shallow, old-fashioned dome with a higher one and redesigned the inner dome, making it semicircular and coffered. From the exterior, they omitted the usual pilaster order, which is found only in the interior. The outer walls of the church of Lapua, built slightly later, received the full Empire treatment: each arm of the cross is borne by Classicist pilasters under a tripartite entablature.

Laukaa Church, designed in 1833, has attracted special interest among Engel scholars in that it has been thought to point the way to a new style, Gothic Revival. Although the church otherwise resembles those of Alajärvi and Lapua, the eight-faced pavilion roof is new, the

Lapua Church.
C. L. Engel,
1827.

external walls have pointed arches, and a rose window is placed above the entrance. Gothic touches in the interior include the two-part domical vault and the pulpit and altar. These features were connected with the Continental interest in the Gothic, which was reflected in Engel's other plans of the 1830s.

Numerous circular churches were designed and built. Plans for octagonal wooden churches were prepared for Kuolajärvi (1828) and the Orisberg mill (1830). The stone church of Nokia was built 1836–38. In shape it resembles the Pantheon plan of Hämeenlinna Church; the most noticeable divergence is the domed tower above the portico. A bell tower was also built for Hämeenlinna Church in the late 1830s.

Hall churches with a west tower were built at Vehkalahti (1826), Ruskeala (1830), Kittilä (1831), Pälkäne (1833), Kankaanpää (1834) and Kymi (1838). The stone church of Leppävirta, built 1846, has a pure Neo-Classical basilican plan. The gallery-framed nave is roofed with a smooth barrel vault, and the altar is placed in a semicircular apse. The stairs to the galleries are in the transepts.

New challenges

After Engel's death, the director of the Finnish building administration from 1841 to 1867 was Ernst Bernhard Lohrmann (1803-70), like Engel a German architect trained in Berlin. During his term of office, the administration was strengthened and decentralized. Eight posts of province architect and province 'conductor' (construction engineer) were established in 1848. The two most prominent new architects were recruited from Sweden in 1852: Georg Theodor Policron Chiewitz (1815–62), appointed architect of the Province of Turku and Pori, and Carl Axel Setterberg (1812–71), his counterpart in Vaasa.

The central administration was also reorganized in 1865: the Intendant's Office was renamed the Board of Public Works, and Lohrmann was the first chief director of the Board for the remainder of his public career. The number of official architects increased, and eventually one could reasonably say that there was a body of professional Finnish architects. Vocational training began in 1849 at the Technical Real School of Helsinki, which changed its name to the Polytechnic Institute in 1872.

No-one has done a comprehensive study of Lohrmann's career yet; his accomplishments in developing the administration and raising the professional standards of architects are known better than his architecture.

In line with the international trend, the precise Neo-Classicism of the Empire period gave way during Lohrmann's time to a more varied, even capricious architecture. Henrik Lilius calls

Villa Hakasalmi, today the Helsinki City Museum. Ernst Bernhard Lohrmann, 1844.

Wooden church of Kerimäki. Adolf Fredrik Granstedt, Axel and Th. J. Tolpo, 1847.

---

this period 'the Age of Disintegrating Classicism'. The phrase stresses the clearly observable fact that Classicist motifs continued to be used, but tectonics, the logical expression of bearing and borne structures, was no longer practised. I myself prefer the 'Age of Historicism', a term much used in the international literature since the 1980s, since it defines the architecture of the latter half of the nineteenth century in terms of the new elements of the period, rather than of what it left behind.

Late 19th-century fascination with the history of architecture no longer focused on the quest for universal formal rules. The rationality and Classical ideals of Enlightenment philosophy gave way to Romanticism, which was obsessed with the irrational concept of authenticity. The focus shifted to the most enigmatic periods of history: in architecture, to the world of Romanesque and Gothic. The forms found there were used freely to attach the desired associations to new buildings. It is easy enough to understand the preference for the architectural forms of the religious Middle Ages in church architecture;

the new combinations of the styles of different periods for both traditional and new secular building types is still a subject of intense scholarly debate. In peripheral Finland, the issue was complicated by the fact that the corps of architects grew rapidly during the heyday of the freely associative, eclectic planning method.

Instead of one highly-educated Engel, the architectural profession now consisted of a mixed bag of architects and master builders with great differences in training and ability. This general point is worth bearing in mind when travelling in Finland and observing with surprise the unexpected austerity or prolixity of a church, townhouse, villa or manor house.

We must confine ourselves here to the work of the best-trained architects of the period, Lohrmann, Chiewitz and Setterberg.

Lohrmann was responsible for the designs of the 'New Clinic', built in the 1850s on Unioninkatu in the centre of Helsinki, the old Post Office (1851) at the foot of the Church of Nicholas, now occupied by the Ministry of Social Affairs and Health, and the low National Mint building (1861) on the Katajanokka shore, today framed by the white cubes of Alvar Aalto's Enso-Gutzeit Building and Olli-Pekka Jokela's Ministry of Foreign Affairs Development Cooperation Department. The Villa Hakasalmi near Töölö Bay, designed 1843–44 by Lohrmann for privy councillor Carl Johan Walleen, is best-

House of Nobility. G. T. Chiewitz, 1862.

known as the home of Walleen's stepdaughter Aurora Karamzin. The elegant mansion, framed by small wing buildings, today houses the Helsinki City Museum, the historical museum of the Finnish capital.

In Turku, Lohrmann's name is associated primarily with the large prison completed on Kakolanmäki hill in 1853: the stark, grey granite facades have done their share to give 'Kakola' its fearsome reputation.

During Lohrmann's period, the longitudinal church plan overtook the cruciform plan in popularity. One of the most impressive of Lohrmann's own works in the field is the whitewashed brick and granite church of Ylistaro from 1847–51. Its massive outline features many Gothic touches, from pointed arches over windows to corner turrets emphasizing the rise of the sturdy west tower. Four columns of wood and four of masonry divide the interior into three aisles.

The planning history of the world's largest wooden church at Kerimäki, still a source of wonder, is still not fully known, but probably master builder Axel Tolpo and his son Th.J. Tolpo built it between 1845 and 1847 to the plans of Adolf Fredrik Granstedt, one of Lohrmann's subordinates. Lars Pettersson's analysis of the stylistic ancestry of the church also provides a general idea of the variety of possible sources at the time for the design of a single country church. Besides the model books at the Intendant's Office, he considers that the designer borrowed motifs from Turku Cathedral, the Hagia Sophia in Constantinople, the Duomo in Florence, the Mausoleum of Theodoric in Ravenna, and Aachen Cathedral. The local builders' personal interpretations of the complex structures drawn by the architect added a further touch.

Ville Lukkarinen associates churches like the one at Kerimäki with the round arch style, also known as Byzantine, Lombard or Romanesque Revival, popular on the Continent at the time. In seeking a new, Prussian style, Karl Friedrich Schinkel sought to combine the Oriental and Classical heritage, to find a synthesis between Greek tectonics and mediaeval vaulting techniques. One assumes that Lohrmann kept his office up to date with developments in the centre of his formative years by acquiring topical literature. Lukkarinen has pointed out that the facades of Koski Church (1867–70) in the Province of Häme were copied from drawings published in Schinkel's *Architectonische Entwürfe* (Architectural Sketches).

The Gothic Revival made its first appearance in the centre of Helsinki in the House of the Nobility, designed by G.T. Chiewitz. The symmetrical facades of the cube-shaped, flat-roofed building are unrendered red brick; the windows are arched at the ends and decoratively

The spacious centre of Loviisa. Town hall in the foreground and church in the background, both by G. T. Chiewitz.

divided with tracery. The facade is dominated by the large paired windows of the second-floor assembly hall; the third floor provides modest, concealed accompaniment. Outwardly, however, perhaps the most obvious model for the House of Nobility is the early Renaissance Italian *palazzo*; the ornamental panelwork of the beautiful assembly hall introduces the appropriate note of mediaeval chivalry.

Chiewitz moved to Finland from Sweden in 1851, producing an impressive oeuvre in the ten years remaining in his life. Employed first in Helsinki and then in Turku as chief architect of the province and town with a private practice on the side, Chiewitz designed a great variety of buildings and drew up town plans; on top of all this, he trained the younger generation in his private 'academy'. Helena Soiri-Snellman discovered among Chiewitz's estate inventory, drawn up after his bankruptcy, a list of the books in his library: he had an extensive, international and very up-to-date collection.

In Turku, Chiewitz's houses added a new building type to the Empire town plan. With its rounded corners, the two-storey house at the corner of Tuomiokirkkokatu and Henrikinkatu blends beautifully with its setting. A light-handed eclecticism brings a novel note to the elevations. The pavilion section of Pinella, Finland's oldest restaurant, located in the cathedral park, still bears traces of Chiewitz's handiwork.

Among the villas of the green island of Ruissalo, the Villa Roma and Villa Haga and possibly others were designed by Chiewitz. He introduced a new international fashion to Finland, the picturesque Swiss style. Chiewitz's asymmetrical villas are divided into several wings, with eye-catching towers, verandahs and gables decorated with lavish wood carvings.

The largest coherent group of buildings by Chiewitz to have been preserved is near the main square of Loviisa. After a fire, the town was rebuilt to a town plan by Lohrmann, ratified in 1858. In addition to a fine church and town hall, Chiewitz designed several residential buildings of stone and wood construction in the centre of town. The church was built of red brick in the Gothic style specified by the parish. The pale, rendered facades of the two-storey town hall are restrained and introverted; the windows hint at the German round arch style. New elements in the housing include the bevelled angles of corner buildings, wrought-iron balconies, streetside doors and greater variation in ground plans.

Chiewitz's town plans gave broad, tree-lined esplanades to Pori (1852), Uusikaupunki (1855) and, finest of all, Mariehamn (1855), the capital of Åland.

As the pet architect of the growing industrial sector, Chiewitz designed factories and housing for several locations. According to Elias Härö,

Vaasa Court of Appeal. C. A. Setterberg, 1862.

at least the Forssa cotton mill, the Littoinen broadcloth mill, the Aura sugar mill, the Tampere linen mill, the Turku ironworks and the Nuutajärvi glassworks employed him. Chiewitz had the international experience that the industrial revolution needed, and was familiar with new construction techniques and building types. The most remarkable testimony to Chiewitz's interest in iron is the transparent cast-iron spire of the Neo-Gothic brick church's tower. Chiewitz and C.J. von Heideken (1832–88) collaborated on the church plans.

The townscape of Vaasa still bears the mark of Carl Axel Setterberg, official architect of the province and the town for almost twenty years. Old Vaasa was destroyed by fire in 1852, and the city was rebuilt on a completely new location. Setterberg's first job on arriving in Finland in 1854 was to draw up a plan for the new town. Setterberg's grid plan, ratified in 1855, featured spacious, planted esplanades to enhance fire safety and to provide an imposing frame for the new town. Another innovation was greater building density than was common during the Empire period. Setterberg thought a varied block structure and two-storey wooden buildings were viable as long as the overall design was sufficiently uncluttered and spacious. Setterberg's town plan served as an example in Sweden, too, where Albert Lindhagen published it in his book of model plans.

Under Setterberg, Vaasa was built up as a Gothic Revival town of Scandinavian stature. Unlike the buildings of Chiewitz, Setterberg's principal works – on which Mirjam Lehtikanto has published several studies – are all close together. They are also very well-preserved: the main public buildings, and above all the New Court of Appeal (completed 1862) have been lovingly restored to their original splendour.

The red-brick Vaasa Church, designed by Setterberg in 1857, has an oblong plan with a west tower. The light colours of the richly panelled interior are accentuated by the abundant daylight entering through high windows.

Industrialization of Finland

Industrialization had an increasing impact on Finnish architecture from the mid nineteenth century on. The textile industry, in particular, rapidly became international, with foreign entrepreneurs and capital streaming in. Inventions in industrial processes, machinery and architecture represented a broader range of international expertise than had ever been seen before in Finland.

Construction for the sawmill and wood-processing industry did not initially give rise to a new industrial architecture: the facilities needed were built of wood using traditional methods.

Verla mill in Jaala, designed by Edward Dippel.

The main monuments to the mighty wood-processing industry of Kymenlaakso (the Kymi Valley) were built in the 20th century; the only remnant of an earlier age is the Verla mill museum in Jaala. The Verla groundwood and cardboard mill was rebuilt after a fire in 1892. The architect Edward Dippel designed the richly varied brick buildings, in which production continued until the 1960s. When the mill closed down, the old machinery and authentic production and working methods were, as it were, embalmed. It is as if the workers were just out for lunch, and work would resume any moment.

Like the wood-processing industry, the textile industry sought out locations where water power was available. The history of the Littoinen broadcloth mill goes back to the 18th century, the Forssa cotton spinnery was founded in 1847, the Vaasa cotton mill in 1865, and the linen mill on the east bank of the Tammerkoski rapids in 1856.

Large, multistorey weaving mills were a completely new type of building. Construction of the large halls needed for machinery was feasible by using new building techniques. The bearing walls of the factories tapered in thickness as they went up. By shoring up the intermediate floors on iron pillars, builders could avoid the necessity for bearing partition walls. A new metal industry sprang up to make these pillars. In the early years, floors were made of wood;

cast iron took over towards the end of the century, and reinforced concrete was introduced at the turn of the century.

An interesting new chapter in the history of architecture was opened recently with studies of industrial architecture. My account is based on the research of Lauri Putkonen. I will concentrate on Tampere, 'the Finnish Manchester', which has an exceptionally monumental industrial complex accumulated over nearly two centuries. Its architectural heritage, abandoned as a result of the structural changes undergone by industry, presents a particularly intricate set of problems from the point of view of urban development and architectural conservation.

The Scottish businessman James Finlayson obtained a licence in 1820 to build a foundry and manufacturing workshop on the banks of the Tammerkoski rapids. He started by weaving woollen cloths and soon expanded to manufacturing cotton yarn. The mill was taken over by St. Petersburg businessmen in 1836 and its output grew. John Barker, who had experience of modern industrial constructions in Belgium, was one of the planners of the first six-storey factory building. The cast-iron columns supporting the floors were made by the new foundry of Fiskars, which had a Scottish foreman. The old mill was enlarged in the 1850s, when the 'Rapids Mill' and the 'Bell Gate Building', decorated with a Neo-Gothic staircase gable, were completed to

Tammerkoski rapids industrial area.

form an imposing main entrance to the factory estate.

Ten new industrial buildings or so were built in the 1870s and 1880s. The most remarkable of these was the 'Plevna', the new weaving shop, built to plans by an English architect but with elevations drawn by the Tampere town architect, F.L. Calonius. The facades were completely unfenestrated: the workshop was lit by skylights in a sawtooth roof. The floor was made of concrete. The weaving shop measured 137 by 39 metres, and provided space for 1,200 machine looms. Finland's first electrical light bulbs were switched on in this building in 1882.

The Finlayson head office and the superintendent's house, 'the Palace', were built in the 1890s to plans by town architect Lambert Pettersson. Construction of the Finlayson estate continued into the 1960s. The close-knit industrial landscape by the rapids was both exceptionally varied and harmonious.

The adjacent Frenckell estate bears witness to the development of the paper industry. The first Finnish paper machine went on line in the whitewashed three-storey mill building in 1844. Industrial paper made of rag pulp rapidly gained ground over handmade paper, and the mill was able to export to St. Petersburg and Tallinn. Even the noted Finnish educator and journalist J.W. Snellman printed his magazine *Saima* on Frenckell mill paper from 1844 on.

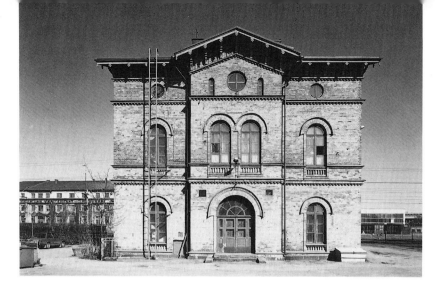

Tikkurila station. Carl Albert Edelfelt, 1862.

The development of groundwood pulp in the 1860s revolutionized the paper industry, and the Frenckell estate was built anew. An octagonal chimney from 1870 has been preserved as a monument to the era. Most of the present buildings were designed by Birger Federley and erected during the first decade of the twentieth century. The mill closed down in 1928 and the estate was taken over by the city. The buildings now contain municipal offices, and the old boiler room serves as the reading room of the public library. A variety of cultural events have been staged in the area.

Development of transport

A network of railways began to reduce travelling times between the cities of Europe in the 1830s. Railway stations became the new, symbolic monuments of the Age of Industry.

Railway construction in Finland began in 1857; the first section, from Helsinki to Hämeenlinna, was finished five years later. The connection to St. Petersburg was completed in 1870, and north-south connections were built at a rapid pace in the following decades. The St. Petersburg line particularly speeded up industrialization in the Kymi Valley: numerous steam-powered sawmills were built to produce goods for the flourishing export trade. Finland had

more track per inhabitant than did the pioneering railway countries Britain and Germany – though only the Norwegian railways covered a smaller proportion of the country than did Finland's.

In Finland the railways were built by the State, with the result that station buildings formed a uniform, hierarchic set of type buildings. The first station buildings on the Helsinki-Hämeenlinna line were designed by province architect Carl Albert Edelfelt (1818–1869).

The first railway station of Helsinki was a stoutish, pale rendered building alongside the tracks, with fairly spare yet varied articulation and ornamentation typical of Historicism. Sirkka Valanto has found prototypes in Germany as well as in Russia. The old station of Helsinki was demolished to make way for Eliel Saarinen's new building in 1918, and the Hämeenlinna station burned down in the same year. Smaller stations were built of either brick or wood. The red-brick Tikkurila station has been preserved as a museum. On the basis of their dominant gablets and abundant wood carvings, the style of the wooden station buildings has been called Swiss; the term 'carpenter style' emphasizes their rich woodwork.

Special carpentry workshops were set up to supply the window frames, doors and furniture needed for the new station buildings.

Stations were divided into five categories in

Pohjois-Esplanadi at the beginning of the 20th century. Theodor Höijer's 'metropolitan' architecture. In the foreground, Grönqvist Building, completed in 1883.

order of importance. Most of the buildings were erected to standard plans. We have no precise knowledge about the designers, but Valanto believes that most of the plans were drawn up by Knut Nylander, who learned his trade from Edelfelt and was appointed architect of the Board of Railways in the 1870s. Bruno Granholm took over this position in 1892.

Railway stations developed into a whole new type of milieu, with engine sheds, depots, warehouses and staff housing built adjacent to the station and interspersed with well-tended trees and bushes. The station buildings also contributed to the development of a range of new forms in wood architecture. Changes in transport in recent years have emptied many fine station buildings, and new uses have been difficult to find.

Theodor Höijer and the growing capital

The first Finnish industrial exhibition, modelled on the great World's Fairs, was held in Helsinki's Kaivopuisto Park in 1876. For this survey of Finnish products, Theodor Höijer (1843–1910) designed a wood-framed pavilion with a floor surface of no less than 7,500 m². The event marked the grandiose culmination of both Finland's industrial development and Höijer's ar-

chitectural career. Höijer was the first properly-trained and talented architect in Finland who did not enter the civil service. He ran a private practice, drawing up plans equally for industry and trade and for new national institutions. In Höijer's lifetime, and largely as a result of his plans, the centre of Helsinki attained a new elegance not too far removed from the appearance of the great cities of Europe.

Höijer received his education at the Technical Real School of Helsinki, then trained under Chiewitz in Turku and under Fredrik Wilhelm Scholander at the Royal Academy of Arts in Stockholm. Upon Chiewitz's advice, he also learned the mason's trade. Eeva Maija Viljo stresses Höijer's practical abilities in her studies of his work: the first commandment of architecture according to Scholander, "God and the middle parts", a Swedish interpretation of the French architectural doctrine of strict symmetry, was well-suited to Höijer's temperament.

Höijer's early years as a private entrepreneur in Helsinki were overshadowed by the famine years of the 1860s. Construction came to a halt. The population of Helsinki in 1860 was only just over 20,000. By 1890 it was over 60,000; the 90,000 mark was passed before the end of the century. The 1880s, in particular, saw the rise of the bourgeoisie: the volume of building increased and construction techniques advanced.

A key element of the economic expansion

was the 1879 Freedom of Trade Act. Culturally, the city flourished with a strengthening of national spirit and internationalization accompanying economic development.

Höijer's commissions in the 1870s included industrial buildings for the Sinebrychoff brewery and plans for a poorhouse, a funeral chapel and an elementary school. The tiny Old Funeral Chapel of Hietaniemi was built 1872 in a modest Romanesque Revival style. Viljo has found the source in a German book of model plans that was already somewhat out-of-date at the time.

The greatest change in the townscape during the last decades of the 19th century was worked by multistorey blocks of rented flats, the first of which Höijer designed in the 1870s. Mariankatu 12, a four-storey apartment block with bevelled corners and a vigorously articulated facade, shows that Höijer took a basically Swedish approach to the fundamental European town building. For the facades, he made free but restrained use of motifs reminiscent of the Renaissance *palazzo*. The most noteworthy feature is the clarity of the overall plan. Over the next twenty years, twelve rental blocks designed by Höijer were built in Helsinki. Some of them, such as Erottaja 2 (1889), have rendered facades sporting boldly palatial sculptural ornament, others are of unadorned brick indicating a new aesthetic of materials (Pohjoisranta 6, 1881). The decorative tendency culminated in the

houses for which Höijer employed the sculptor Robert Stigell to make figurative compositions. At the corner of Erottaja and Uudenmaankatu, muscular Atlantes sculpted by Stigell support a corner bay.

The block-length business palace which industrialist Fredrik Wilhelm Grönqvist commissioned Höijer to build was larger and more expensive than any previous private building project in FInland. With the building of the Grönqvist House from 1880 to 1883, the townscape of Helsinki took a big step in the direction of Vienna, Paris, Berlin and St. Petersburg. The largest residential flats in the house followed international models of wealthy urban living. The doors to the high, spacious streetside rooms – salon, dining room, gentleman's study and bedroom – formed an enfilade. The less important rooms and staircases adorned with decorative paintings were pulled back onto the courtyard side.

Three years later, the Hotel Kämp was completed on the adjacent plot. Hidden behind a more restrained facade, the luxurious restaurant, staircase and hall of mirrors were the principal rendezvous for the notabilities of the Finnish business and art world for many decades. The memory of the Kämp lives on even though the building was demolished in the 1960s and replaced by a new bank office with some copying of the old building. From time to time, nos-

talgia rears its head: the bank has been asked to turn the hall of mirrors into a restaurant once more.

To complete the fine row of houses on Pohjoisesplanadi, Höijer finally designed a building with an elegant restaurant in the adjacent block for the confectioner Catan. He then made way for younger architects. Blocks of flats by Höijer in various parts of town were demolished up to the 1960s because their ornamentality offended the Modernist aesthetic of authenticity. Especially when comparing old photographs of Mannerheimintie to the present situation, the architecture buff is gripped with nostalgia. Fortunately, many generations are now concerned with preserving the cosmopolitan atmosphere of Esplanadi: the park has become a rendezvous particularly favoured by young people.

Höijer also designed a great variety of public buildings. The range of his assignments reflects the growing affluence and increasingly lively cultural scene of Helsinki. The volunteer fire department on Keskuskatu has been pulled down, but the red-brick main fire station's tower, reminiscent of the city hall of Berlin, still dominates the rise of Korkeavuorenkatu, the library on Rikhardinkatu has been beautifully renovated, and the Ateneum on Rautatientori (Railway Square) was raised to new glory as the National Art Museum in 1990.

The Fine Arts Association of Finland and the Finnish Society of Crafts and Design had long hoped for a building to house their schools and art collections. The prime mover of the Ateneum project was Carl Gustaf Estlander, professor of aesthetics, whose pet theme was instruction in arts and crafts. After long years of preparation, the plans drawn up by Höijer in 1884 were adopted as the basis for construction. His plan fitted in the industrial art institute and its collections, the Fine Arts Association's drawing school and art collection, and a library and auditorium. Höijer's first plan was judged too expensive, and a pared-down proposal was approved in 1885. The symmetrical building was in a Renaissance style in keeping with its programme. The central staircase leading up to the exhibition rooms on third floor provides a dignified focus for the building. Communications in the two lower storeys were arranged so as to permit the use of classrooms as exhibition space if necessary. Separate entrances to the schools flank the central bay.

As Eeva Maija Viljo points out, the main facade of the Ateneum was an exceptionally ambitious one in Finland. At Senator Leo Mechelin's wish, Höijer drew sketches for sculptural decoration focusing on the large window of the Fine Arts Association's studio in the building's central mass. The ornamental programme included both the great international masters of art and the symbols of Finland. The sculptures

Corner of Torikatu and Malminkatu, Joensuu.

were made by C.E. Sjöstrand and Ville Vallgren. Placed above the main entrance, Raphael, Phidias and Bramante stand for painting, sculpture and architecture; in the pediment, the Maid of Finland rewards industriousness in arts and crafts with laurel wreaths. Since the Ateneum was inaugurated in 1887, many appeals in Finland's quarrelsome art world have been made to the motto under the pediment, *Concordia res parvae crescunt* (Concord makes little things grow).

Fin de siècle

Until the end of the 19th century, stone houses more than two storeys high were rare among the low wooden houses in towns other than Helsinki, Turku, Tampere and Viipuri. Apart from churches, the odd fine town hall, a number of schools and a handful of central hospitals and prisons represented historicist monumental architecture in Finland's smaller towns.

The town hall of Kuopio was designed by F.A. Sjöström and completed in 1883. The town hall of Tampere was built in 1890 to plans by Georg Schreck on a market square site designated in the 1779 town plan. Both are in Germanic Neo-Renaissance style with a broad, dominant central avant-corps.

The discipline of the Empire period was abandoned in the architecture of wooden houses around the middle of the century. The busy economic activity of the period also enlivened life in the wood towns. Shops were opened, housing was built for tenants, and courtyard storehouses were built bigger than before. Building types were more varied, and their architecture appreciably pluralistic. The historicist influence of the bigger stone houses is in evidence from the 1880s on. Facades were divided into fields, horizontal and vertical sidings were used in combination, boards were sawn to a variety of profiles, windows were large, and a new, T-shaped frame division was favoured. A multitude of carved and sawn decorations made their appearance. Local masters developed their own styles: some copied the railway stations with their Swiss style and gablets, others produced amusing imitations of Renaissance *palazzo* details in woodwork. In a thoroughgoing study of the building of the town of Joensuu from 1848 to 1890, Henrik Lilius showed what a variety of motifs could be fitted into just one small town.

According to Viljo, more than sixty Lutheran churches were built between 1870 and 1895, about two thirds of them of wood. The most appreciated material, however, was bare red brick, which was used for churches in towns and

Joensuu Church.
Josef Stenbäck, 1903.

in the country. The basic type had a basilican plan with a tower at the west end in a mixture of Romanesque and Gothic styles. Romanesque forms predominated in Tampere's Messukylä Church, designed by Höijer in 1879.

The pointed arch only came into fashion in the 1890s. Helsinki built the grand Neo-Gothic Church of St. John in 1891 to plans by the Swedish architect A.E. Melander, with two west towers as in mediaeval cathedrals. The wooden church of Kajaani, designed by Jac Ahrenberg (1847–1914), had a fine Gothic Revival interior with a structure echoing the forms of mediaeval wood architecture.

Some of the Neo-Gothic churches have been pulled down. The fine timber church of Lahti was designed by August Mellin and completed in 1890 on a hilltop site from which it dominated the town; it was demolished in 1977 to make way for a church designed by Alvar Aalto. More commonly, the varied interior woodwork of churches has been smoothed over: thus, the interior of the red-brick church of Mikkeli, designed by the most prolific Finnish Gothic Revival church architect Josef Stenbäck (1854–1929), was simplified in the 1950s to plans by Martti Välikangas. In Joensuu Church (1900–1903), Stenbäck combined cast cement parts painted in a light shade with red brick.

During the directorship of Axel Hampus Dahlström (1829–82) from 1870 to 1882, the mo-

nopoly of the National Board of Public Works on architecture ceased. International architectural competitions were arranged for the most important public buildings. The competition for the Bank of Finland, held in 1875, resulted in victory for the Berlin architect Ludwig Bohnstedt. His bank palace, in Italian Renaissance style, was completed in 1883. The next competition was held 1877 for the planning of the Surgical Hospital. Although all of the prizes went to foreign architects, the commission was awarded to Sjöström, a Finn. As was the custom of the times, he made free use of the prize-winners' designs in his pavilion-like plan for the hospital, which was completed in 1888.

When the Diet began to convene regularly in the 1860s, the commons urgently needed a place of assembly; the nobility, of course, already had their own building. After a great deal of manoeuvring, an architectural competition was held 1881 for a building to be erected on a site behind the House of Nobility. The winner was F.A. Sjöström, but new complications arose, and eventually both the site and the architect changed.

As the result of a second competition, Gustaf Nyström (1856–1917) was commissioned to design the House of Estates across the street from the Bank of Finland. Nyström's building, completed in 1891, heralded a new stylistic phase in public building in Finland: the dignified clarity of Viennese Classicism.

*House of Estates.
Gustaf Nyström,
1891.*

The precisely shaped cube of the House of Estates is dominated by the pediment of the central portico, displaying a sculptural group made by Emil Wikström – as the result of another competition. A frieze painted along the top of the smooth walls was originally intended to be replaced by a sculptural frieze designed by the architect. The interiors of the House of Estates have just been restored to their original glory. The abundant decorative painting of the ceremonial staircase and the large halls gleams like new, and the smaller rooms have been refurbished for Council of State banquets.

Before his work on the House of Estates, Nyström had already designed the nearby State Archives, completed in 1890. In 1883, when he was a 28-year-old novice, he received the commission directly from the chief archivist. Having obtained a Senate grant for the purpose, Nyström made a careful study of modern library and archive buildings in Sweden, Germany, Britain, France and Austria in preparation for the assignment. The State Archives was a thoroughly up-to-date building, combining a bold use of modern building techniques with a solidly Classicist appearance. Nyström paid special attention to fire safety and lighting, solving these problems by completely separating public spaces from the storerooms. The stacks were placed in a closed, separate wing at the back of the plot; the research rooms occupied another, rectangu-

lar wing; and the offices were placed along a linking corridor. The plan was based on a 'warehouse system'. According to Ville Lukkarinen, the plan was so newfangled that when presenting it Nyström thought it necessary to point out that he had made his choice on the basis of examples set by the national libraries in London and Paris.

For many decades, critics argued that the Rationalist iron structures of the State Archives conflict with the building's Classicist exterior. During that time, the architecture of the 1890s was judged on Modernist principles, which automatically required new forms for new technology. Lukkarinen has convincingly shown that Classicism and light, modern structures were two ingredients of Nyström's consistent Rationalist approach. The old building is sandwiched between two annexes today, but its uncompromising clarity can still be seen if one follows Nyström's plans on a tour of the building.

From the 1880s, Nyström was the most influential Finnish practising architect and instructor. He graduated from the Helsinki Polytechnic Institute in 1876 and continued his studies under von Ferstel in Vienna. He then immediately launched into a teaching career at the Polytechnic, first as lecturer of structural engineering, then as senior lecturer of architecture; he was the leading Finnish teacher of architecture from 1885 until his death in 1917. In 1903,

State Archives, research room. Gustaf Nyström 1890.

he was appointed head of the whole institute. Nyström was also active in municipal politics, proposing innovations based on international examples.

Nyström worked as 'court architect' for the University of Helsinki, desinging new buildings and annexes to old ones. In this work, he gave proof of his sensitivity to the *genius loci*. Within the Empire-style centre, his respect for the basic rules of Engel's architecture was absolute; in more peripheral areas, a newer idiom was acceptable. The rotunda of the annex to the University Library, built 1902–06, smoothly blends the latest discoveries in steel construction with the new stylistic features of Art Nouveau and Engel's harmony of proportions.

Helsinki's covered market, completed 1889, combines steel structure with a cheerful wall pattern of red and yellow brick: modest modernity was appropriate for a commercial context. In the Nordic Union Bank offices, built 1898 on Aleksanterinkatu, Nyström produced the first Finnish facade built entirely of fieldstone: the granite elevations expressed the security of the bank's operations.

As the country's leading instructor, Nyström made a wide-ranging contribution to architectural training, which always remained a technical discipline in Finland: no division into a technical institute and art academy ever took place. Nyström was the very embodiment of this Germanic tradition, and proved its worth in both his work and his teaching.

Women entered the architectural profession at an early stage in Finland. The Polytechnic Institute of Helsinki, set up when the Technical Real School was dissolved in 1879, accepted women as special students from the beginning. Signe Hornborg received her architect's diploma from the Polytechnic in 1890, the first woman in Europe to do so; even in the United States, only one woman is known to have been admitted to the profession before her. Between 1887 and 1908, twenty-nine women studied at the architecture department of the Polytechnic: eighteen of them graduated. Nyström's general pragmatism seems to have played a major part in this development. By 1908, when the institute became the University of Technology, the presence of women students was a matter of course.

*Tampere's Church of St. John,
today the Cathedral.*

The twentieth century

Finnish history and the new style

*The mediaeval night was a beautiful night, full of
dreams and radiant visions. Its life is like a fairytale
to modern man, its dreams like the hymns of saints.*

ARMAS LINDGREN

Between 1871 and 1902 the Finnish Antiquarian
Society organized eight expeditions of student
architects and scholars to document the country's oldest architecture. They produced a collection of over 3000 drawings and watercolours,
in the final years also photographs. Armas Lindgren's picture of a wooden church (reproduced
on page 45) was painted during one of these
journeys. The Archaeological Bureau (founded
1884), the precursor of the present National
Board of Antiquities and Historical Monuments, furthered the expeditions as a systematic
project of scholarly research, museology and architectural conservation.

   The architect Yrjö Blomstedt and Victor
Sucksdorff made a journey to eastern Karelia in
summer 1894. The resulting anthology of illustrations, *Karjalaisia rakennuksia ja koristemuotoja* (Karelian Buildings and Ornamental
Forms) consisted of photographs and drawings
presenting the rich forms of Byzantine-style
wood architecture. The movement to idealize
the Karelian 'Land of Song', which had begun

with the collection of folk poetry, now had an architectural monument as well.

From 1902 on, Gustaf Nyström's courses also included compulsory trips to various parts of Finland to make dimension drawings of old buildings. *Arkitekten* journal reported in 1916 that extensive material on rural and urban architecture had accumulated in the University of Technology collections. Exhibitions were held; some even dreamed of founding a museum of architecture.

The Finnish architectural heritage – the sturdy monuments of the Middle Ages and the modest wooden churches and grey timber buildings of later centuries – were an important part of the world of the architects who came of age in the 1890s. The young architects had discovered their Finnish roots, and felt that these roots were strong enough to raise Finland to the forefront of international modernity. They were equally passionate in their national and international orientation.

The young architects travelled widely, acquainting themselves at international exhibitions and congresses with town planning, housing design, technology, hygiene and industrial art. They read international publications, primarily German and Austrian but also French and British. Not many of them actually crossed the Atlantic, but they were also familiar with American novelties through books and periodicals.

The Finnish architectural profession had grown considerably by the turn of the century: there were over 100 architects throughout the country. Private practice prospered, since work was plentiful.

In 1892, the Architects' Club was founded as part of the Technical Society. It drew up rules for architectural competitions and arranged discussions about fees, construction techniques, building ordinances and current projects. The trade journal *Arkitekten* was founded in 1903.

The minutes of Club meetings and the prolific writings of architects provide a comprehensive record of ideas in the air at the turn of the century. In an analysis of architectural writings between 1890 and 1910, Ritva Wäre concluded that the architects were not consciously striving to create the specifically Finnish style cherished by latter-day National Romantic thought. Their goal was a new style, free from historicist ballast and in harmony with both modern construction techniques and the national heritage.

In fact, *Art Nouveau* is the most appropriate epithet for Finnish architecture at the turn of the century. National Romanticism was a major ideological ingredient of the new architecture, but not an adequate general appellation. The much-used term *Jugend* is also misleading, as it points exclusively to Germany. Belgian-French Art Nouveau, the Vienna Secession and the British Arts and Crafts movement all had a significant

Olofsborg housing company, Katajanokka, Helsinki. Gesellius, Lindgren, Saarinen; 1902.

impact in Finland. Especially the development of handicrafts and industrial art, in which architects were closely involved, was based on the ideas of John Ruskin and William Morris. The conception of art as the common denominator of the whole environment and the striving for the *Gesamtkunstwerk* was particularly well-suited to Finland, where industrialization, after all, lagged far behind Britain and western Europe.

The busy construction business and lively cultural scene of the turn of the century provided an ideal ground for varied architecture. The public sector built several major institutions and arranged numerous design competitions. Towns grew; schools and churches were built throughout the country. Finnish Art Nouveau took on a distinctly local character in housing construction.

Gesellius, Lindgren, Saarinen 1896–1905

The collaboration of Herman Gesellius (1874–1916), Armas Lindgren (1874–1929) and Eliel Saarinen (1873–1950) began in 1896, and quickly resulted in an artistic breakthrough. Albert Christ-Janer has recorded Saarinen's words: "Before we had completed our courses at the school even we had won two prizes. Then during our first years in our offices, we received

an unbelievable amount of commissions."

The trio first came into the public eye in 1897 by winning a competition for the design of a block of flats to be built by the merchant Julius Tallberg in Helsinki's Katajanokka district. A peninsula adjacent to the old centre, Katajanokka had an old-fashioned, straightforward town plan, but the apartment blocks built at the turn of the century turned it into Helsinki's most unified Art Nouveau district. The sharply angled Tallberg plot offered the young architects the perfect setting for their Romantic stylistic ideals. They produced a four-storey castle that dominates the townscape with a sculpturesque outline made up of a high roof, a corner tower, abundant bays and architectural detailing. The effect is reminiscent of the atmosphere of historical novels rather than of any specific existing precedent.

The granite ground floor contains small businesses and provides a solid foundation for the Tallberg House. The three residential storeys contain one spacious flat each with a floor plan based on a new brand of residential planning emphasizing domesticity and family privacy. The irregularly shaped rooms were grouped so as to provide a variety of views, lighting effects and colour contrasts.

Kauppakatu, Tampere's main street of the new architecture, was built about the same time. In their plan for the Tampere Savings Bank,

*Hvitträsk,
Kirkkonummi.
Gesellius, Lindgren,
Saarinen; 1903.*

Gesellius, Lindgren and Saarinen took the mul-
tiformity introduced in the Tallberg House
one step further. However, the corner tower,
planned as a particularly modern feature, was
not built.

Gesellius, Lindgren and Saarinen continued
to develop the sculpturesque housing block in
their next Katajanokka houses. Olofsborg
(Kauppiaankatu 7, 1901–02) and Eoli (Luot-
sikatu 5, 1902–03) – like the 'Physicians' House'
on the corner of Kasarmintori square, completed slightly earlier – were characterized by massive bays and high tile roofs. Particularly delightful interior features include the skilful woodwork and metalwork of doors and fixed furnishings, ornamental paintings, and stained-glass
staircase windows.

Presenting the Physicians' House in *Ateneum* magazine in 1901, Bertel Jung wrote that
the architects "... erased the word 'apartment'
from their vocabulary, replacing it with 'home'.
They banned the phrase 'the facade requires',
instead saying 'cosiness requires'. They forgot
the traditional measurements for windows and
doors, they forgot conventional ornament and
room disposition. Committing themselves to
obeying nothing but the strict, prosaic building
ordinance and traditional ideas about what goes
to make up a flat, they seized upon the task with
youthful enthusiasm, building outwards from
the inside."

Gesellius, Lindgren and Saarinen won second prize in the 1898 competition for the facades
of the Finnish National Theatre, but this time
the commission went to Onni Tarjanne (1864–
1946), who had already designed the floor plans.
His design gave the theatre a form blending features of famous European playhouses with elements showing American influence; the facades
are massive granite. The theatre was completed
in 1902 at the north end of the Railway Square.
Eliel Saarinen later paid beautiful tribute to the
theatre in his plan for the main railway station.

Large apartment blocks in the new style
were designed for Katajanokka by other architects as well. The finest include the Aeolus
House (Satamakatu 5, 1903) and the Wellamo
House (1904), visible from far out at sea on its
Vyökatu corner site. Both were designed by
Selim A. Lindqvist in a somewhat less massive
style than that of the great trio. Soon the style of
the leading architects was also applied in the
area by master builders, whose sometimes highly original decorative ideas became objects of
architects' scorn; later generations, however,
have gladly accepted them as amusing ingredients of a unique setting.

For the young architects of the turn of the
century, however, the modern block of flats was
only the second-best kind of home. Their ideal
was the private house built in nature's lap. Numerous villas designed by Gesellius, Lindgren

Hvitträsk. Photo: Loja Saarinen.

and Saarinen according to the new philosophy were built in the surroundings of Helsinki. The most perfect embodiment of their ideals was Hvitträsk, built 1901–04 for the architects themselves. Despite damage suffered in a fire, Hvitträsk – now a museum – offers the most authentic introduction to their dreams.

Saarinen's contribution to Hvitträsk's design has been emphasized, partly because most of the final drawings were by him and partly because he lived there longest, until his move to the United States in 1923.

The architects found the site of their dreams on the steep shores of Lake Hvitträsk, in the heart of a spruce forest. The earliest sketches for a house are in Lindgren's sketchbook. The main body of the building, with the homes of Saarinen and Lindgren and the studio between them, was placed right on the brink of a cliff; the second wing on the other side of the courtyard contained Gesellius's home. The main complex stands on a high stone foundation, with the upper storeys built of corner-jointed round logs. The steeply pitched roof is faced with red tiles. In 1922, the massive, dominating log tower and the adjacent Lindgren wing were destroyed by fire.

The best-preserved interior space consists of a series of rooms grouped around the large, hall-like main room in Saarinen's home, truly "the home as a work of art", as the title of a book about Hvitträsk puts it. The rooms, varying in

size and shape, the multitude of materials used, the mellow colours, the gentle interplay of light and shadow, the fixed furnishings and textiles – all these gave expression to the pivotal ideals of the period.

Gesellius, Lindgren and Saarinen rose to international fame with the Finnish Pavilion at the 1900 World's Fair in Paris, another commission resulting from victory in a competition. The planners were limited by the dimensions specified by the French organizers and the Board of Industry's order to use simple forms and light materials. The structure of the pavilion was wood, and the main portals were carved of granite and soapstone, but the walls were built of light materials and the decorations were made of plaster, as more durable materials would have been too expensive.

Eliel Saarinen bore the main responsibility for the plans, and also supervised construction of the pavilion in Paris. The building was in the shape of a rectangle rounded at one end, with a high tower with vaults, which had frescoes on subjects from the Kalevala, painted by Akseli Gallen-Kallela. The interior design and exhibits were rather varied, but the overall effect was more harmonious than that of other pavilions. Although elements were borrowed from sources as distant as the United States and Austria, the clarity of the design, flavoured by decorative motifs from Finnish nature, was enough to at-

Finnish pavilion at the Paris World's Fair, 1900. Gesellius, Lindgren, Saarinen.

Pohjola Insurance Company. Gesellius, Lindgren, Saarinen; 1901.

The customer service room of the Pohjola building was like a stately farmhouse interior.

tract favourable international attention. The experience taught Finns what a significant role architecture can play in shaping a nation's image. The Paris pavilion became a legend which inspired many later Finnish projects abroad.

The Finnish press revelled in the pavilion's 'Finnishness'. I.K. Inha's description in the *Kyläkirjaston Kuvalehti* ('Village Library Illustrated') reflected the defiance of Finns under Russian oppression: "The pavilion's shingled roof suggests the steep shingled roofs of our ancient stone churches. The walls and windows are reminiscent of our original rural homes – 'stone barns' – according to one observer. The external decorations vividly bring to mind the Finnish wilds. Sullen bears lumbering at the foot of the tower, bears' heads and squirrels decorating the arches of the main corridor, giant pine cones supporting the towers that flank the main corridor, lily pads on the outer walls – all these depict the fauna and flora of our country. The material of the walls stands for granite, of which Finland has an endless store. The ribs of the tower dome depict the sun's shimmering rays – a symbol of the light of the north, which never goes out on summer nights, and of the bright hopes of a nation unbroken even by the severest trials…"

The greatest architectural symbol of Finnish culture is the National Museum. A plot had been acquired for the building in Töölö, and the Board of Public Works had submitted drawings based on a typical Classicist museum plan for Senate approval when the young generation of architects took up arms. The pamphlet *Vårt Museum* (Our Museum), signed by the architects Herman Gesellius, Bertel Jung, Armas Lindgren, Harald Neovius and Lars Sonck, was distributed to members of the Senate. In text and illustrations, the pamphlet presented recent European museums which "sought to transform the cultural-historical museum from an assortment of wares, boring to most viewers, to an inviting sanctuary". A good museum was defined as a building in which every age has a space of its own – reflecting its specific character and distinct from all others – and formed of a spatial system disregarding symmetrical axes, through which each visitor can wander according to his own tastes. The pamphlet called this plan type an agglomerative system.

The Senate yielded and in 1901 announced a planning competition, in which victory went to Gesellius, Lindgren and Saarinen. By and large, their plan lived up to the description given in *Vårt Museum*. The building's facade, consisting of rough boulders, brought together a whole range of historical motifs. The building nestled right up to Mannerheimintie, leaving the remainder of the spacious plot free for later additions.

Armas Lindgren was in charge of this assignment. His sketchbook shows the development

of the plan, which divided up the building into sections twined about two courtyards. The official drawings were approved in 1905; the foundation stone was laid the following year.

In December 1905, Gesellius, Lindgren and Saarinen wound up their joint practice. Of the office's uncompleted projects, Lindgren, who had been artistic director of the Central School of Applied Arts since 1902, took on only the National Museum. Construction was a long-drawn-out process: the amount of stone used for the facades was cut down, and the granite intended for the walls of the main hall was replaced by whitewash. The museum was not completed until November 1910; even after this, the planning of the courtyard, its buildings erected in numerous stages, and its encircling wall kept Lindgren busy for many years.

During their ten years together, Gesellius, Lindgren and Saarinen had not actually worked together on all their assignments. The studies of Marika Hausen and Tytti Valto have revealed that in some competitions they each sent in individual entries. The collaboration was a fortunate phase in the young men's lives which enabled them to unite their various strengths in a rich final result in many plans. The scope and international importance of Eliel Saarinen's later career raised him into a heroic class of his own, which is why all too often he has received sole credit for many of the trio's joint projects.

From Romanticism to Rationalism

The rich Romanticism of Gesellius, Lindgren and Saarinen was not the only Finnish architectural style at the turn of the century: the technical rationalism of Gustaf Nyström also made headway. The leading master of reinforced concrete and structurally based plans was Selim A. Lindqvist (1867–1939), who set up a private practice in 1888. His Mercury Building (Pohjoisesplanadi 33, 1890) brought new terseness to the streetscape dominated by Höijer's Renaissance Revival. The engineer Elia Heikel devised a system of columns permitting an exceptionally open plan for the two bottom storeys, and Lindqvist composed the facade in the new international style, with dominating windows, cast-iron columns and granite pilasters.

The Lundqvist Building at Aleksanterinkatu 13, completed in 1900, has been called Finland's first real business building. Assisted by Heikel, Lindqvist placed the frame of the building on cast-iron columns so as to provide maximum flexibility for alterations in the interiors. The facade is merely a protective curtain wall; the architecture expresses the structure of the building. The building lost its original character when it was later converted into a department store.

In general, too much of Selim A. Lindqvist's architecture in Helsinki has been destroyed. The

Lundqvist Building, Selim A. Lindqvist, 1900.

Nordic Bank facade stone in the courtyard of the Museum of Finnish Architecture.

Jugendstil touches he assimilated in Germany in the 1890s once dominated much of Helsinki's central townscape. The best-preserved examples are the small Villa Johanna on Laivurinkatu (1905–06) and the Villa Ensi (1910) nearby on Merikatu.

The conflicting architectural tendencies of the turn of the century collided most violently at the corner of Aleksanterinkatu and Mikonkatu, when Gesellius, Lindgren and Saarinen designed the facades and principal interiors of the Pohjola Insurance Company's commercial and residential complex between the Lundqvist and Mercury Buildings in 1899–1901.

The Pohjola Building was as romantic as the Lundqvist Building was rational. The insurance company's function and its name, suggestive of the Kalevala epic, prompted the architects to adopt a castle-like monumentality and National Romantic sculptural decoration, for which a newly-discovered material, Juuka soapstone, offered the perfect medium. The facade articulation was clearly based on the style of the American architect H.H. Richardson, though critics stressing the domestic sources of the ornamenta-

tion have tended to overlook this international influence. The main entrance, embedded in a niche, is guarded by grinning monsters and a group of bears carved by Hilda Flodin. The abundant wood carvings and wrought iron work complement the dynamically spiralling stair hall. Anna-Liisa Amberg interpreted the strange creatures depicted in the carvings as the diseases mentioned in the verses of the Kalevala, or "the bastards Stitch, Bloat, Gout, Rickets, Boil, Scab, Cancer and Plague, born with the Mistress of Pohjola as midwife".

The main public space became a poetic, rural interior – a *pirtti*; the load-bearing iron column was hidden inside a Byzantine wooden shell, and most of the walls were covered with pine panelling. The main interiors have been preserved, though unfortunately the fixed furnishings have been moved elsewhere.

The wild era of sculpturalism and asymmetric volumes soon passed. For the Nordic Bank on Unioninkatu near Senate Square, Gesellius, Lindgren and Saarinen designed stone facades of a very different kind in 1904. The plan was governed by axial symmetry, with granite slabs forming smooth surfaces accentuating separate decorative elements. The ornamental motifs were international, with more than a touch of Wiener Moderne and directly influenced by the Swedish architect Isak Gustaf Clason (as Marika Hausen points out). This architectural landmark

Suvilahti power plant, Helsinki. Selim A. Lindqvist, 1908.

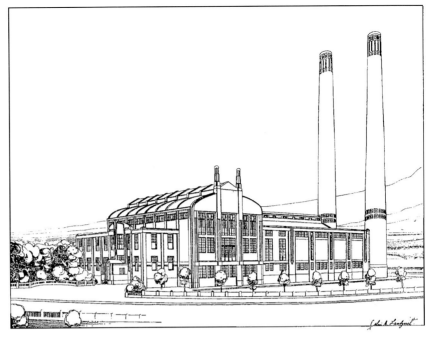

Helsinki Railway Station, Eliel Saarinen, 1904–19.

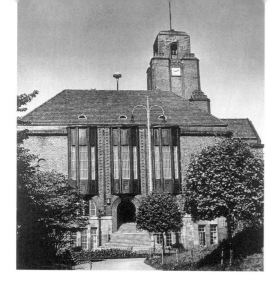

Lahti Town Hall.
Eliel Saarinen, 1912.

was pulled down in 1934, and the facade stones were used to build the embankment for a marina. One of the stones gathers moss on the courtyard lawn of the Museum of Finnish Architecture.

An impassioned debate broke out between the Romantics and the Rationalists after the results of the architectural competition for Helsinki's new railway station were published. Eliel Saarinen won the competition with a plan showing ponderous granite facades terminating in fortress-like towers and gables, and lavish ornamentation with eight bear sculptures as its most conspicuous elements. The jury praised the noble overall effect of the plan, but Saarinen's planning principles met with devastating criticism in the pamphlet "Architecture; a manifesto dedicated to our opponents", written by Gustaf Strengell (1878–1937) and Sigurd Frosterus (1876–1956), who had both taken part in the competition.

Strengell and Frosterus cruelly dissected the entire Romantic architectural and literary output of Gesellius, Lindgren and Saarinen. Quoting Otto Wagner, they demanded a realistic consideration of the needs and potential of the age, and opposed the use of historical motifs. They furiously proclaimed the inseparability of architecture and engineering, and pointed out that architecture is not a pictorial art. Their polemic ended in an appeal: "We want a brawn-and-

brain style for railway stations and exhibition buildings. We want a brawn-and-brain style for business buildings, theatres and concert halls!"

Sigurd Frosterus had worked at the office of Henry van de Velde in Weimar, Strengell at the office of C. Harrison Townsend in London. Their demands for an international modernism arose from these experiences. Strengell's railway station entry is lost, but Frosterus's dynamic plan 'Eureka' fulfils the programme of their manifesto.

Saarinen took the criticism seriously: 1904 marked a turning-point towards Rationalism in his career. When the final drawings for the station were completed in 1909 after several intermediate phases, the influence of Frosterus was quite obvious. The clear spatial arrangement, economic arched concrete structures and precision of detail made the Helsinki Railway Station, which was inaugurated in 1919, a monument which has defended its position in the history of world architecture.

The principal monument of the Rationalist or Constructivist movement, however, was indubitably Selim A. Lindqvist's Suvilahti power plant, built in two phases in 1908 and 1913. The architecture lays bare the building's pure reinforced concrete frame. Lindqvist also designed several smaller electrical stations around Helsinki, the Kallio fire station and the Töölö tram depot. The new utilitarian architecture reflects the arrival of international innovations in Helsinki, the increased comfort of everyday life, and a generally more dynamic lifestyle.

In Mikkeli, Lindqvist designed the town hall by the main square (1912) as well as the Naisvuori water tower (1911), in which the reinforced concrete water drum and its supporting pillars were left visible. Elsewhere in Finland, water towers still tended to be dressed up in red brick to make them look like historical towers.

After the Railway Station, Eliel Saarinen specialized in town planning, influencing the development of the centre of Helsinki in many ways. He planned and campaigned for a new thoroughfare leading east from the Railway Square, the present-day Kaisaniemenkatu, drawing detailed streetside elevations and toying with plans for an opera house to be built along the new street. On Keskuskatu, the street heading south from the Railway Square, he designed a shopping arcade which runs through a whole city block.

Few administrative offices were built in the early years of the century, but two of the finest are the red-brick town halls designed by Eliel Saarinen for Lahti (1912) and Joensuu (1914). Both have a soaring, stepped tower; Lahti Town Hall formed a handsome counterpart to the church at the other end of a long street axis. The architecture of these buildings shows a general return to disciplined symmetry.

In Armas Lindgren's architecture, the 1910s marked a clear return to Classicism. At the foot of Desprez's church on the main square of Hämeenlinna, he designed a terrace with pavilions connected on both sides by a colonnade. He also designed a covered market in similar style at the lower end of the square, but it was not built. The Skogster Building, a red-brick residential and commercial block completed nearby in 1914, showed that Lindgren's Classicism was closely related to new developments in Swedish and Danish architecture.

In Helsinki, Lindgren won a competition for the elevations of the Suomi Insurance Company's new office building. The granite form of his entry virtually meant a return to the world of the Renaissance *palazzo*. Engel's Old Church across the street obviously influenced the design as it matured through numerous preliminary phases.

Lindgren's monumental series of buildings in Helsinki culminated with the Kaleva Insurance Company offices, built as an extension to the New Student House in 1914 and containing the Seurahuone hotel and restaurant. Here the architect had the opportunity to add to the monumental townscape formed by the National Museum and Railway Station as well as producing an exquisitely detailed interior plan for business and entertainment needs. At the development stage, Lindgren deleted a corner tower – which

Staircase in the Kaleva Building.

Kaleva Insurance Company offices, Armas Lindgren, 1914; New Student House, Lindgren and Wivi Lönn, 1910.

had already gone through numerous transformations on paper – and hid the faces of the roof with a continuous, crenellated cornice. The exterior received an unusually articulated smooth granite facing.

The interior shows the Viennese inspiration behind the building's strict aestheticism. Except for the street level, the main business facilities have been lovingly preserved, but the restaurant has lost its worldly refinement, for which Lindgren is thought to have sought inspiration as far afield as the renowned Hôtel Negresco in Nice.

Lars Sonck

Of the young turn-of-the-century architects, Lars Sonck (1870–1956) is well-loved as an exuberant poet of wood and stone. During a long, gregarious and energetic life, he left his stamp on many areas and periods of Finnish architecture, but his most impressive achievements came early in his career.

Sonck took part in the expeditions of the Antiquities Society and won his first major architectural competition while still a student. As a result, he was commissioned to design St. Michael's Church in Turku in 1894. The red-brick church was not completed until 1905, by which time its largely Gothic Revival form no longer satisfied Sonck, especially as the dense, small-scale urban development he had hoped for around the church was never built, and the church was left to stand alone on its hilltop site.

Sonck always aimed at the 'total work of art', and wished to plan everything from the town plan to the tiniest furnishing detail. He worked together with a host of artists and craftsmen. A church was to be both an organic element of its setting and its crowning glory. Sonck came closest to this ideal in St. John's Church in Tampere (the present-day Cathedral), which he was commissioned to design after winning a competition in the year 1900. From the beginning, Sonck insisted on granite as the facade material, and in the spacious ground plan he combined mediaeval vaulting with the plans of modern American and British preaching-houses of his day.

St. John's Church, completed in 1907, developed into a synthesis of a variety of international ideas and a highly personal vision of Finnish architecture. Sonck simplified the tower into a variation of the church tower of Finström, his native village in the Åland Islands. The masonry for the facades was dressed using the squared-rubble technique, which Hugo Lindberg had presented in great detail in a lecture at the Technical Society following a study trip to Aberdeen in 1898.

Sonck issued careful instructions for the expressive finish of the rectangular blocks of grey granite from Kuru. As the research of Paula

Lasse's villa,
Finström.
Lars Sonck, 1895.

Kivinen has shown, the church is a monument to the tremendous *tour de force* accomplished by the stonemasons of Tampere. The stone wall and gate structures framing the church are built of rough, undressed fieldstone; the granite surface is smoothest in the internal walls and ornamentation. The finesse of the plan is shown by the fact that the granite was polished in two places only, the chancel screen and the top of the altar.

The interior is dominated by a vast stellar vault with a span of 16 metres and borne by sturdy granite piers. The pew railing echoes the outline of the vault, underscoring the altar's centrality. The broad pews and transepts are overshadowed.

The effect is completed by Valter Jung's sculptural decoration, Hugo Simberg's extensive frescoes and stained-glass windows, and Magnus Enckell's altar fresco and stained-glass chancel window.

Sonck won a town plan competition for the area surrounding St. John's in 1902 but again, as in Turku, the capricious mediaeval web of blocks that he aimed at was never built.

Sonck's townscaping ambitions were finally brought to fruition in 1912, when Kallio Church in Helsinki was completed. By this time, Sonck's style had taken a turn towards symmetrical monumentality, and the church formed the dominant element of the long perspective formed by Unioninkatu and its continuation, Siltasaarenkatu. The visitor is surprised by the modest domesticity of the interior, which does not meet the expectations aroused by the granite facades and the steeply terraced rise.

Sonck's turn-of-the-century style is represented in Tampere by the Tirkkonen Building, completed 1901 and designed in collaboration with Birger Federley. The ground floor was faced with Ylöjärvi granite, with rendered brick for the upper storeys. The two lower storeys were intended for businesses, and featured such modern inventions as pneumatic mail chutes.

The Helsinki Telephone Company building in Korkeavuorenkatu, completed on a steeply sloped site in 1905, was the most important application of Sonck's stone architecture to a modern assignment. Pekka Korvenmaa has analysed the architectural principles on which the commercial building was based and the conflict between its modern function and the mediaeval references of its facade. Sonck worked on the building at the same time as on St. John's Church, and was obsessed with the rubble masonry facade at the time. He had no particular wish to express the building's business function in the exterior: at the time, this seemed a pointless Historicist convention.

In Helsinki's Eira Hospital (1905), Sonck abandoned the conventional ground plan based on symmetrically ordered wards, seeking to pro-

Helsinki Stock Exchange. Lars Sonck, 1911.

vide a new cosiness by means of variation. Outwardly the hospital building was in tune with the adjacent villa district.

The Mortgage Bank Building on Etelä-Esplanadi, completed in 1908, marked the beginning of a new period in Sonck's architecture. With its smooth granite stonework, the facade is solemnly symmetrical. A free-standing portico as the dominant facade motif became Sonck's favourite theme, repeated in a number of later buildings, including the red-brick block of flats at Maneesikatu 2b (1909) and the Keskuskirjapaino printing works at the corner of Bulevardi and Erottaja (1913). Sonck's longest variation on the same theme brought him victory in the planning competition for the facade of the Helsinki harbour warehouses in 1911. The reinforced concrete frame, the largest in Europe at the time, was designed by Selim A. Lindqvist. This palatial warehouse, which is over 140 metres long, was recently converted into a hotel.

The Helsinki Stock Exchange, completed on Fabianinkatu in 1913, has sternly handsome granite facades concealing a well-lit indoor courtyard leading up to the offices and restaurant. The design, unique in Finland, bears witness to the impression made by H.P. Berlage's Amsterdam Stock Exchange and Martin Nyrop's Copenhagen City Hall, both much-discussed in Finnish professional circles at the time.

The general Finnish admiration for Karelian wood architecture did not lead to the construction of copies of old Karelian houses. The most obvious loans were the use of round logs and decorative motifs suggesting Karelia for summer villas. One might also detect touches of the Norwegian *drakenstil* in their gables, bargeboards, doorsills and window sills, a reflection of Finnish emulation of the land of fjelds and fjords and its outdoor way of life.

Lassebo (or Lasse's villa), built by Lars Sonck in his home parish Finström in 1895, met all the requirements of the new ideals. Located on a rocky seaside site, its foundation is laid of large fieldstones and its walls built of round logs with sculpturesque highlighting of the corner joints. A Karelian-type balcony nestles in the shelter of the gable overlooking the sea. Originally the scenery could also be taken in from the round bull's-eye windows of the porches. The villa was the fabled setting for summer parties for the Finnish and Scandinavian architects' corps.

One of Sonck's most ornamental wooden villas was the Villa Hällberg, completed in Mariehamn in 1896 and today serving as the local yacht club's pavilion. Most of his villas were built on out-of-the-way coastal or forest sites, and their peace was only intended for family and friends.

By 1911, when Ainola was built in Tuusula as the composer Jean Sibelius's home, Sonck's extravagant Art Nouveau period was over. The

TAMPERE, Palotorni
TAMMERFORS, Brandtornet

Tampere main fire station. Wivi Lönn, 1907.

only Karelian memories in the house, which has light, painted vertical weatherboarding, are the wide, balconied gable and the frames of the small-paned windows; otherwise it is not too far removed from Swedish villas of the same period. To be sure, the summer villa spirit would not have suited this house, intended as it was for year-round living. Sonck went on designing log cabins for summer use until the 1940s. According to Korvenmaa, he basically remained faithful to solutions he had devised at the turn of the century.

Kultaranta, built 1913–16 for the Naantali businessman Alfred Kordelin, has been used for many years as the summer residence of the Finnish president. The grandiose granite palace with a large garden and park was designed for a nouveau-riche bachelor who wished to entertain Finnish high society in flashy international style.

Wivi Lönn

Wivi Lönn (1872–1966), who received her architect's diploma from the Polytechnical Institute in 1896, is honoured as Finland's first female architect. In fact four women architects graduated before her, but she was the first to set up her own office. Her first major commission was the Tampere Finnish Girls' School, built 1901–02. She rejected the conventional central corridor plan in favour of a type of plan she had seen in new school buildings during a study trip to England and Scotland. The meandering building contains a variety of pleasant spaces, with cosy entrance halls leading to the classrooms. The windows and attractive decorations are typical Art Nouveau.

Lönn later designed dozens of schools throughout Finland, three of them – the Alexander Elementary School (1904), the Tampere Home Economics School (1905) and the Tampere Business Institute (1913) – in her home town.

When Lönn won the design competition for Tampere's main fire station in 1906, the jury held her entry to be far and away the best, particularly praising its flexibility in combining different types of spaces. Parts of the curving brick frame had sculpturesque granite facing, and a well-proportioned tower completed the aesthetic effect. Later alterations have affected the architecture somewhat.

Well-considered ground plans were a distinctive feature of Lönn's architecture. This skill came into its own in her collaboration with Armas Lindgren.

Lönn's and Lindgren's joint entry won the planning competition for Helsinki's New Stu-

Eira villa town.

dent House in 1908, mainly on the strength of the clever interlocking of the student union's assembly rooms with more mundane spaces in two wings. The facades were largely based on Lindgren's Pietinen Building, a large block of flats completed in Viipuri in 1907. The preserved drawings of the Student House plan show that Lönn took care of the spatial and structural planning, while Lindgren concentrated on the facades and the abundant decoration. The New Student House was a fine monument to student life in central Helsinki. Sadly, its unique interiors have been destroyed.

The collaboration of Lönn and Lindgren continued in the planning of the Estonia Theatre in Tallinn. At the inauguration of this large playhouse and concert hall, the speakers thanked Mr. Lindgren for the excellent floor plans and Miss Lönn for the beautiful ornamentation. In his response, Lindgren (Lönn was not present) told the surprised audience that their roles had been the exact opposite of this. Renja Suominen-Kokkonen, the author of the most recent study on Lönn, points out that Lönn's talent was in direct conflict with the ideas of the time about what constitutes men's and women's work.

A handful of villas in the Tampere region bear witness to Lönn's ability in the field of romantic timber architecture. Her extensive later output included work for an industrial estate at Säynätsalo near Jyväskylä, where the factory manager Hanna Parviainen, an advocate of reform, asked Lönn to carry out a variety of building assignments.

The new urban ideal

The impression usually made by the modern small town is uninviting, monotonous and rigid. And yet people rarely give a second thought to this; at most they explain the impression of tedium with the smallness of the town. But if we think of the pleasant impression made by almost any mediaeval town, no matter how small and irregularly built, even those with only the humblest of buildings, we must surely seek the defects of the modern small town elsewhere than in its insignificance. Could not its dullness be due to the way it is planned, divided and built?

Thus began Lars Sonck's article "The Planning of Our Small Towns", published in *Ateneum* journal in 1901. He could see nothing good in open towns built to grid plans. He felt that even the drunkenness rampant in small towns could be ascribed to the cheerless, ruler-drawn environment.

Sonck had experienced a revelation when reading the Austrian Camillo Sitte's *Der Städtebau nach seiner künstlerischen Grundsätzen* (City Planning According to Artistic Principles, 1889), which awakened him to the idea that a

Munkkiniemi-Haaga plan, aerial perspective. Drawing by Eliel Saarinen, 1915.

whole town could be a unified work of art if artistically trained architects could wrest urban planning from the engineers drawing their straight street lines.

Sonck's first influential article on town planning, "Modern Vandalism: Helsinki's Town Plan" (published 1898), applied Sitte's approach to Helsinki. It sparked off heated controversy among architects, engineers and local authorities and, most importantly, resulted in the first Finnish town planning competition, announced in June 1898. The competition area was the Helsinki district of Töölö, located near the centre but unbuilt until then because of its awkward, rocky terrain. From the perspective of the new town planning ideals, the area was ideal.

The young architects – Sonck, Bertel Jung and Valter Thomé – submitted picturesque, Sittean entries, whereas their professor Gustaf Nyström, together with the engineer Herman Norrmén, drew up an entry based on straightforward axial compositions. After a great deal of wrangling, Sonck and Nyström were jointly commissioned to draw up the final plan, which was ratified in 1906. It was a compromise, reflecting Sonck's bold visions only in the curving lines of a few streets and in a handful of minor details.

Around the turn of the century, the role of architects in urban development strengthened in two ways. Town planning competitions were held for entire towns or parts of them; gradually, the towns themselves woke up to their need for permanent town planning architects.

Bertel Jung's (1872–1946) active approach to his job as Helsinki's first town planner from 1908 on served as a model for all of Finland. Jung worked hard at devising a variety of tools for controlling urban development in detail. He worked out his methods during construction of Etu-Töölö ('Fore Töölö'), in dealing with the problem of workers' housing, and above all in the development of Vallila district. His office issued byelaws in support of town plans, different town districts each receiving their own. Internal building restrictions within blocks were established for Töölö in order to keep space for courtyards. Inspections of elevation drawings were stepped up, and gradually a set of pattern elevations was drawn up, to be observed by architects as closely as town plan directives.

To back up the plans for individual districts, Jung also soon introduced master planning. His urban ideals changed little by little, as his early idealization of the Middle Ages was superseded by more Classical models, Sitte by the Englishman Raymond Unwin and the German Werner Hegemann. Jung's farsighted approach enabled the Finnish capital to prepare in advance to tackle issues which were urgent at the time only in the largest cities of Europe and the United States; by international standards, Helsinki only

Kuningasavenyy, principal motif in the Pro Helsingfors plan by Eliel Saarinen and Bertel Jung, as envisaged by Saarinen.

really became a city after the year 1900, when its population reached 100,000.

Jung sketched a first master plan for Helsinki as early as 1911, including in it a broad green belt starting from Keskuspuisto (Central Park), which begins on the two sides of Töölö Bay.

In 1910, Eliel Saarinen started work on planning a new town district for the extensive lands acquired by the M.G. Stenius company in Munkkiniemi and Haaga districts, then northwest of the Helsinki city limits. The project was based on expectations of major growth in the capital region. It was a utopian effort to produce an urban environment of high aesthetic quality on the one hand; on the other, it was one of the gigantic financial speculations typical of the pre-war era.

Saarinen had already tried his hand at major urban planning in his plans for Canberra, Budapest and Tallinn. The Munkkiniemi-Haaga plan, published in handsome book form in 1915, presented a clearly differentiated town with public buildings placed at the intersections of boulevards, housing in the centre in high blocks with large courtyards, and fringe areas slated for low-rise housing of great variety. Only two buildings from Finland's greatest urban utopia were ever carried out: the Munkkiniemi Casino, which now serves as the governmental Administrative Development Agency, and a small row house in Hollantilaisentie.

Saarinen included a tentative draft for a master plan of Helsinki in the Munkkiniemi-Haaga plan. He continued work on this plan together with Bertel Jung; their 'Pro Helsingfors' plan was completed in 1918. It can be thought of as a newly independent state's optimistic vision of the future, based on forecasts of stupendous growth. The plan shows port facilities spreading out along both sides of Helsinki peninsula, with a ring of satellite towns providing land for industry and housing within quick reach of the centre.

The plan showed the entire Helsinki peninsula as a densely-built metropolis. The main railway station was to be moved to Pasila; Töölö Bay would be reclaimed. A narrow urban railway and the broad, tree-lined Kuningasavenyy, or King's Avenue, would lead to the central core, with the last vestiges of Jung's central park on either side, softening the impact of its penetration into the tight web of closed blocks. The name and dimensions of Kuningasavenyy manifested the desire of Finns to raise Helsinki on a par with the great cities of Europe. The street would have shifted the city's emphasis from Senate Square, the centre of Czarist power, replacing the static, symbol-laden open space with the throbbing pulse of a boulevard.

The first city district to be built according to the new town planning principles was Helsinki's Eira. The decision to develop a villa town on the hill south of Tehtaankatu was taken in 1905.

Lars Sonck drew up the first town plan for the Kulosaari villa town in 1907; Armas Lindgren designed the row house complex which was built in 1917 on a slope descending to Kluuvi Bay.

Bertel Jung, Armas Lindgren and Lars Sonck spontaneously drew up a town plan proposal, on the basis of which the city engineer prepared the town plan, which was ratified in 1908. The streets, clinging to the hilly site, had softly curving lines, and a square with a sea view to the south was laid out in the centre of the area. Eira was to have been the new model district, with private houses placed on verdant garden plots within limits set by the town plan and byelaws. The regulations were not strict enough, however, and the district filled up with small apartment blocks, as critics were quick to point out. In an article published in conjunction with the Munkkiniemi-Haaga plan in 1915, Gustaf Strengell condemned Eira as an example of total failure. Later generations, however, have disagreed, and the district is now one of the most highly valued in Helsinki.

Several bourgeois villa towns, based on the new international housing ideals, were built outside Helsinki in the early 20th century, usually along railway lines. Heikki Waris has counted no less than 21 companies or societies engaged in land speculation in the Helsinki suburbs between 1895 and 1930. The suburbs of Haaga, Kulosaari and Kauniainen were built up around 1910.

The development of Kulosaari began in 1907, when a group of architects, engineers and businessmen established the Ab Brändö Villastad and bought up Kulosaari, an island of some 250 acres east of Helsinki. Lars Sonck, one of the founders, immediately set about to draw up a town plan. The network of roads and narrow streets was determined by the terrain contours and the shoreline. Sonck staked out spacious plots for large houses along the shore to provide as many people as possible with access to the sea and the sun. He placed the public buildings in the middle of the island, at its highest point.

Later the plots had to be split up, as few could afford to buy so much land. The founders' houses were not large, either; a new, modest domesticity was their chief wish. The delightful wood villas of Lars Sonck, Armas Lindgren and many others have made way for denser settlement, and one can only try to reconstruct the original ambience from scattered fragments. One of the best-preserved fragments is the land around Kluuvi Bay, consisting of low-rise housing scattered about a fine park, with adjacent public buildings and an axial composition of row houses designed by Lindgren on a slope.

Especially in Helsinki, workers' housing was a matter of common concern for architects and welfare authorities at the turn of the century. The State and the city wrangled about financial responsibility, but gradually it began to be recognized that private enterprise could not produce housing for all those in need of it. Studies

revealed the wretched conditions in which the poor lived.

A town plan was drawn up in 1908 for a part of Helsinki known as Old Vallila, where workers were encouraged to build wooden homes to model plans. Despite the carefully prepared building byelaws, the area did not develop into a Shangri-La of pleasant private houses; instead, as the welfare board discovered, Vallila became a troubled district of cramped tenement houses. As a result of thoroughgoing renovation, however, Vallila has become a popular address in recent years. Charming wooden houses on plots shaded by large deciduous trees form a small town idyll right near the centre of town.

Independent Finland

The First World War brought to a halt the favourable economic development of Finland's last years under Russia. Once life in the newly-independent state had settled down after the turmoil of civil war, however, the economy revived rapidly, and the foundation for a modern industrial state was laid in the years between the wars. Finland had the fastest industrial growth in Europe during this period. The international depression in the early 1930s halted this trend briefly, but soon production was on the rise again. The wood-processing industry dominated in the 1920s, the paper industry took the lead in the 1930s, and the metallurgical industry expanded in the late 1930s.

The dynamics of the economy regulated the construction business. During industrial boom periods, companies built entire towns, employing the country's best architects to design production plants as well as the communities which sprang up around them, from housing to churches and from clubhouses to bank offices.

The volume of housing construction fluctuated. In the early 1920s, Finnish towns suffered from a severe housing shortage. Government subsidies for housing production increased gradually, as did private construction. The prewar peak in building was not reached again until 1923, but this was followed by a dramatic increase brought to an abrupt halt by the depression of 1930.

Until the 1960s, urbanization proceeded slowly, though a steady stream of people moved south and to the principal towns. Town dwellers accounted for only 15% of the population around 1910. The 20% mark was reached in the 1930s; not until the early 1970s did the urban population overtake the rural population.

When Finland became independent in 1917, most of the nation's 38 towns were small. The combined population of Helsinki and its suburbs was over 200,000; Turku, Tampere and Viipuri had some 50,000 inhabitants each. The larg-

est town in Ostrobothnia was Vaasa, with a population of 30,000.

For many years, urban scale remained modest. Only in Helsinki did multistorey commercial and residential blocks form entire city districts; Turku, Tampere and Viipuri had such buildings only in the very centre. Elsewhere, single-storey wooden houses were still the norm and tall stone buildings rare exceptions, even in town centres. According to Heikki Waris, in 1930 Helsinki had 1301 buildings four storeys high or higher. The ten next biggest towns had only 505 buildings of this size altogether.

Architecture became a university discipline in 1908, when the Polytechnical Institute was renamed the University of Technology. The head of the faculty until 1917 was Gustaf Nyström, whose Classicist approach had alienated students even in the early years of the century. Nyström's successor was Armas Lindgren, who had a fundamentally different attitude to history. Lindgren encouraged his students to study the architectural strata of Italy, accumulated over the centuries, and the austere yet abundant forms of their local environment.

Study trips to Italy were all the rage in the 1920s. The young architects' sketchbooks show that the monuments described in guidebooks were no longer the main attraction: they focused on anonymous alleyways, humble vernacular architecture and the rolling countryside. The beautiful sketches of Hilding Ekelund and Erik Bryggman pay the finest tribute to the landscape and long-lived culture of the south. They also show the importance of Italy's *architettura minore* to the new Nordic Classicism and, by extension, to Functionalism.

Finland gained independence from Russia in 1917. In its early years, the young republic concentrated on strengthening its Scandinavian ties. Finns took every opportunity to distance themselves from their former overlords. In analysing architectural trends, one should bear in mind that Swedish and Norwegian models were eminently practical, quite apart from their aesthetic fascination. To be sure, Finnish architects adopted a variety of innovations directly from the big cities of the Continent, but for many everyday problems a Swedish precedent could be found for a way to adjust a more southerly idea to the harsher conditions prevailing in the North. This was particularly true of urban planning and housing construction.

The history-minded young architects of the 1920s particularly admired Finland's Swedish period: the Classicist official buildings and workers' housing of the 18th century. Scandinavia's first international exhibition and congress on urban development, held in Gothenburg in 1923, elevated the Swedish mill village, as an example of model architecture of the past, to the level of Europe's historic townscapes.

Parliament House, designed by J. S. Sirén, is the most important public building of the independent republic; its heart is the elegantly designed round assembly chamber.

Among the Swedish architects of the 1920s, the Finns admired Ragnar Östberg and Carl Westman, and later particularly Gunnar Asplund. Details from the standard house plans of Osvald Almqvist can be found in workers' housing in Finnish industrial communities, and *Praktiska och hygieniska bostäder* (Practical and Hygienic Housing), a Swedish committee report from 1921, has been found among the effects of many a deceased architect and municipal official.

Nordic Classicism

The architectural style of the 1920s could be called double Classicism. Architects favoured forms derived from Graeco-Roman Antiquity for ground plan composition as well as for the articulation of surfaces. They sought inspiration in ever earlier historical periods. The old tradition of Classical details provided a vocabulary attaching a whole range of associations to architecture. The basic forms favoured in 1920s architecture were a more intangible manifestation of Classicism. The main principles of composition – even in buildings with little Classicist surface decoration – were the axial symmetry of intact geometric forms, the repetition of identical building parts and numerical relationships based on the golden mean. This Classicist core was the

foundation from which the Modernist movement sprang.

In the course of the 1920s, Classicist ornament thinned out. The final phase produced a reduced, or abstract, form of Classicism. Architects made eclectic, sometimes ironic, use of the old rules of proportion and decorative motifs.

The most important Finnish architectural project in the early years of independence was the new Parliament House. Three architectural competitions, a long debate on location, and a building assignment of unprecedented complexity preceded the inauguration in 1931 of the solemn granite fortress designed by J.S. Sirén (1889–1961) on a rocky site in Töölö. Sirén started work on the final planning stage in 1925, concentrating solely on this assignment, incomparably his most important work and the last and most perfect total work of art produced by Finnish Classicism.

The competitions established the basic plan, with a round assembly chamber at the heart of a straightforward, cubic mass. The other facilities were placed around the assembly in a strict but logical hierarchy. The main change to the competition entry was the exterior, which was faced entirely with granite. The abundant use of marble, stucco and hardwood in the interior corresponded to the hierarchy of spaces.

The chamber constitutes the nation's symbolic heart. The members' desks form the

Helsinki Art Hall. Jarl Eklund and Hilding Ekelund, 1928.

The City of Helsinki's Finnish-language workers' institute was designed by Gunnar Taucher and completed in 1927, the annex by Aulis Blomstedt in 1959.

ground level. Highest up sits the Speaker, who is elected by the members from their own ranks. The Government, which enjoys Parliament confidence, sits between the two levels. Columns mark off the public galleries. The iconography is of ecclesiastical precision. Highest up in the chamber, in a position comparable to images of saints in a church, stand sculptures by Wäinö Aaltonen symbolizing Finnish labour and the country's future.

Of the public buildings erected in Töölö in the 1920s, the Helsinki Art Hall (1928) stands in marked contrast to the Parliament House. Jarl Eklund drew up the initial plans in 1917; Hilding Ekelund (1893–1984) was the principal author of the final plans. The Art Hall, with a plan based on a combination of symmetrical and asymmetrical elements, is as light and unassuming as the Parliament House is heavy and ostentatious.

The Tampere City Library was designed by the brothers Jussi (1886–1962) and Toivo Paatela (1890–1962) and built on the west bank of the Tammerkoski rapids in 1925. The architects designed the new cultural institution near Bassi's church and Engel's bell tower, taking the form of Engel's Helsinki University Library as their model. The town of Hämeenlinna converted its old Russian garrison church into a Classicist city library in 1924 to Bertel Strömmer's plans, which called for demolition of the tower and

modernization of the interior and exterior.

The Compulsory Education Act of 1921 sparked off an extensive construction programme throughout Finland: an average 150 schools were built every year. Small, rural elementary schools were most in demand, and the desire to ensure their architectural quality resulted in a demand for standard plans. An architectural competition was arranged for the purpose in 1921, and the booklet "Architectural plans for rural elementary schools" was published the following year. Thus, the leading architects of the capital left their imprint on the remotest parts of Finland: the Classicist wooden buildings of the period are beautiful monuments to the ideal of universal education. The old school buildings, deprived of their function by rural depopulation, offer a curious sight to the traveller driving along small country roads. Some are deserted; others provide studios and accommodation for artists, craftsmen or writers.

The finest elementary schools in the country were designed by Gunnar Taucher (1886–1941), Helsinki's city architect. The first of these was Käpylä elementary school (1929), the most up-to-date was Vallila's elementary school for Swedish-speaking children (1932) and the largest was the Aleksis Kivi School on Brahenkatu (1934). Taucher's schools and Workers' Institute (completed 1927) were clean-lined buildings with classrooms placed in a row along a

corridor, preferably on one side only to provide the best possible lighting.

The five-storey central elementary school of Kotka was built 1929 to plans by Kaarlo Borg (1888–1939). The vigorous plan is complemented by pale rendering and exceptionally elegant Classicist decoration.

The National Board of Building produced Classicist school plans well into the 1930s, introducing a solemn note to many a Finnish town. With their rendered or bare red-brick facades and composition based on even-sized classrooms on symmetrical axes, these schools bear a distinct family resemblance. Even in a strange town, any Finn will recognize the tall, palatial lyceum flanked by a spacious, empty courtyard.

The architecture of private schools provided more variety. Elsa Arokallio (1892–1982) designed the green schoolhouse of the Helsinki Girls' Senior Secondary in Kruunuhaka district, in which numerous reliefs adorn the corridors. The Private Swedish Girls' School (1929) on Apollonkatu in Helsinki, designed by Eva Kuhlefelt-Ekelund (1892–1984), is one of the pearls of Finnish Classicism. The playful Italian references and free composition lend an atmosphere of refinement to the whole area.

Church builders were busy throughout the 1920s. Gripped by the fever of local patriotism, even small villages erected fine temples. Some eighty parish churches were built in Finland between 1910 and 1939. Industrialists paid for churches built in their factory villages, turning them into independent parishes. Hanna Parviainen financed the construction of Säynätsalo Church in 1926, Walter Ahlström did the same for Noormarkku Church (begun in 1929) and Gösta Serlachius for Mänttä Church (1928). The first two were designed by Armas Lindgren and the church in Mänttä by W.G. Palmqvist.

The typical church of the 1920s had an oblong plan with a west tower. The group includes a variety of structures large and small, built of wood, brick, even concrete. The wooden churches usually had vertical weatherboarding, the brick churches were rendered with facings of varying thickness and coarseness. The colour scale was pale and restrained, ranging from shades of grey and yellow to pink, as in Säynätsalo. In reaction to the Gothic Revival churches of the late 19th century, now in disfavour, fairface brick was rarely used for exteriors. Here as before, Lars Sonck made a stand against the mainstream with his red-brick Mariehamn Church (1927), St. James's Chapel in Paimio (1929) and Mikael Agricola Church in Helsinki (1935).

A growing appreciation of the Finnish countryside may account for the popularity of references to the 18th century during this period. While offering respect to the setting of the church, architects took pains to assert its posi-

*Muurame Church.
Alvar Aalto 1929.*

*Taulumäki Church,
Jyväskylä. Elsi Borg,
1929.*

The densely built Helsinki district of Etu-Töölö surrounds the rocky outcrops of Temppeliaukio.

tion as the principal monumental building of the community. When Yrjö Sadeniemi (1869–1951), working for the National Board of Building, designed the wooden church of Pelkosenniemi in Lapland (1927), he made it the undisputed dominant feature of the hillside village. The New Church of Iisalmi, built 1934 to plans by Eino Pitkänen (1904–1955), soars from the highest elevation of this town of hills, a landmark visible from afar.

Dreaming of a new Tuscany in central Finland, Alvar Aalto gave Muurame Church (1929) a delightful Italian accent on a hillside site. Töölö Church (1930), designed by Hilding Ekelund at the head of a long ascent, brought a whiff of Italy to Helsinki. The original interiors of both churches were modest to the point of plainness. The fine black-and-white interior of Muurame has been destroyed in later repairs.

Jämsä's old cruciform church, designed by the Intendent's Office in the 1820s, burned down in 1925. Kauno S. Kallio (1877–1966) made the new church so similar to the old one that, together with the old bell tower that was saved, it could easily be taken to be a hundred years older than it really is at first glance. Kallio defended his church, which was completed in 1929, by pointing out that the old church had the best possible scenic location, and the form of the cross was best-suited to both the landscape and the old bell tower. The sensitive articulation and ornamentation typical of the final stage of Nordic Classicism characterize the interior.

Elsi Borg (1893–1958) won the design competition for Taulumäki Church in Jyväskylä with a plan that emphasizes the height of the hill site with a clean-lined stepped gable which may reflect the influence of Copenhagen's famous Grundtvig Church. The varied detailing, warm colours and rural ornamentation give the interior a highly individual character.

The harmonious townscape

The 1920s were years of intense urban development in Finland. The turn-of-the-century ideal of the city as a total work of art took new form under the Classicist banner. Extensive European and American precedent gave rise to the big-city model, for which Eliel Saarinen's Munkkiniemi-Haaga plan had helped pave the way.

Instead of variety and sculptural whimsy, planners sought classical harmony. They dreamed of magnificent, straight boulevards and closed blocks of uniform height adapted to the width of the streets, with corner towers to highlight the most important crossings. Even sky-

scraper plans were put forward for the corner of Esplanadi and Mannerheimintie in Helsinki. Public buildings, trade and even industry still had their place in the town plan of the 1920s, correctly placed in close proximity to residential buildings.

Everyday housing comforts were furthered by planning joint courtyards inside blocks, planting them to provide sheltered gardens and playgrounds with access from all stairways. Only a few gateways led to the courtyard from the street. Björn Linn has used the term *storgårds-kvarteret* ('large courtyard block') for this type of block structure.

Before the Town Plan Act of 1932 came into force, building ordinances were the main tool of urban development. Swedish models were followed in dealing with many issues. The inadequacy of legislation did not prevent clarity in planning when this was a priority.

As Helsinki's town planning architects, Bertel Jung and his successor Birger Brunila (1882–1979) carried out numerous small-scale planning projects, modern traffic plans and housing areas. The 1924 town planning competition for the centre of Helsinki produced entries which looked fine on paper but were never implemented. The most impressive achievements of the Classicist urban ideal were harmonious residential areas.

The final town plan of Etu-Töölö was rati-fied in 1917 in a form streamlined by Jung. The dignified red-brick owner-occupied apartment buildings of the new district were built mainly in the late 1920s. The facades of the houses of Töölö do not tell the observer whether the evenly-spaced windows conceal one-room flats or patricians' dwellings with five or six rooms. The great frame depth of the buildings called for a variety of hall plans. The architecture was related mainly to the large housing blocks of Copenhagen, although Töölö lacks the Danish capital's large, planted courtyards. The residents insisted on fencing off their plots, although Jung opposed this to the last.

Jung had more reason to be satisfied with New Vallila, a workers' area for which he had drawn up the plans around the same time. With its large courtyard blocks and new, narrow-framed stone houses behind facades based on model elevations, it was the most uniformly Classicist of Helsinki's new town districts. Both houses and apartments followed Swedish innovations of the period, the most significant source being Albert Lilienberg's contemporaneous 'governor's house blocks' in Gothenburg although, unlike its model, Vallila was built entirely of rendered brick.

The first block courtyard set the pattern for the whole district. This was block 555, a block of workers' apartments designed by Armas Lindgren and Bertel Liljequist. The house was origi-

*Careful planning made New
Vallila a dignified, harmonious
district. A key element in the plan
was a block designed 1916 and
after by Armas Lindgren and
Bertel Liljequist as housing for
the metallurgical company
Kone ja Silta Osakeyhtiö.*

*Block 555 has the most spacious
and attractive courtyard in the
whole of Vallila.*

Atrium block of flats and Hospits Betel, the termination of Kristiinankatu in Turku. Erik Bryggman, 1927 and 1929.

Jyväskylä Workers' Club. Alvar Aalto 1929.

Tampere Technical Society building, containing the Tammer Hotel. Bertel Strömmer, 1929.

Wood Käpylä. Martti Välikangas, 1920–25.

nally intended to consist of flats for the workers of a large metallurgical company, but it was completed as a municipally subsidized joint-stock company in 1929. The Hauho and Sture housing companies, designed by Martti Välikangas (1893–1973), are also among the most attractive buildings in the area, with light, idiosyncratic ornament adding the finishing touch to the rhythmic architecture.

Mäkelänkatu was built to Gunnar Taucher's plans as Vallila's splendid main artery. The full length of the three-part city rental block at Mäkelänkatu 37–43 was completed in 1926. The handsome ensemble of columns and entablature framing the central portal reveals the original intention of the town planners to bring in a new street to meet Mäkelänkatu at this point. However, the opposite side of the street was later developed as an ungainly industrial complex.

The architecture of Heinrich Tessenow and Gunnar Asplund was in favour among Finnish architects in the 1920s. Combined with an admi-

ration for Italy, this was evident not only in Taucher's buildings but in the youthful works of Alvar Aalto and Erik Bryggman as well. Bryggman designed the large residential blocks Brahenkatu 9 (1924), Kellonsoittaja (1925) and Atrium (1927) in his home town Turku. All have smooth rendering and windows with six or eight panes brought up right to the wall surface and with slight variation in the frames. To the first-floor windows Bryggman liked to attach sturdy balustrades; together with the fine door frames, they accentuated the rise of the walls.

The Atrium house is in three stepped parts on a sloping plot on Yliopistonkatu. Together with the Hospits Betel opposite, it constitutes Finland's most Italianate townscape. Following a trip to Germany in summer 1928, Bryggman moved on from Classicism to pure Functionalism in the Hospits design. This did not produce a jarring effect, however, as all the components of the ensemble developed together harmoniously.

Of the many bleak housing blocks of the period, Alvar Aalto's Väinönkatu 44 in Jyväskylä (1924) is among the most ascetic. In contrast, the almost contemporary Jyväskylä Workers' Club (1925) took on an all but palatial character. The elegant details were long concealed beneath later commercial paraphernalia, but the recent decision to protect the building is bound to redress these errors eventually.

In the Jyväskylä Defence Corps Building,

completed in 1929, Aalto reduced Classicism to subtle hints, adding a distinctive touch to the pure form of the building with a broad ornamental band reaching up to the cornice. The Southwestern Finland Agricultural Co-operative Building in Turku (1927–28) was another major work bordering on Functionalism, with delicately Classicist interiors which have inspired a variety of scholarly interpretations.

Tampere's city architect Bertel Strömmer (1890–1962) was responsible for much Classicist architecture in his home town. The fine Tuulensuu Building on Hämeenkatu (1929) contained an attractive cinema, and the Technical Society Building (1929) housed the Tammer Hotel and its elegant restaurant. The two-storey apartment buildings in Palomäentie on Pyynikki hill brought dignity to working-class living.

The Käpylä garden town in Helsinki was built 1920–25 to mitigate the housing shortage and financed mainly by municipal subsidies. Martti Välikangas designed the houses, which were built of prefabricated wood units, and placed in accordance with a town plan by Birger Brunila and Otto-I. Meurman. Puu-Käpylä, or 'Wood Käpylä', combined the British idea of the garden town with the traditional Finnish wooden town and the most popular models of the Swedish small house industry to form a pleasant environment. Plans to raze the houses in the 1960s in order to make way for apartment

blocks foundered against the opposition of building conservationists; following recent renovation, Puu-Käpylä is now one of the most desirable districts in Helsinki.

Functionalism

International Modernism made its triumphal entrance into Finnish architectural debate and competitions under the name of Functionalism in 1928. The young generation condemned Classicism as a masquerade, demanding modern technology purified from historical ballast in response to the new challenges of the modern age. They hailed the achievements of Bauhaus in Germany and the buildings and writings of Le Corbusier as harbingers of a new era. They swarmed to Sweden to view the works of their colleagues Gunnar Asplund, Sven Markelius, Sigurd Lewerentz and Uno Åhren. Raija-Liisa Heinonen gives a detailed account of this turbulent period in her study on the breakthrough of Functionalism in Finland.

In summer 1929 the city of Turku arranged a large-scale trade fair to celebrate its 700th anniversary. The fair architects, Erik Bryggman and Alvar Aalto, turned the event into a manifesto of orthodox Functionalism. The fairground plan was based on the principles of the German Siedlung movement, and the buildings proved that

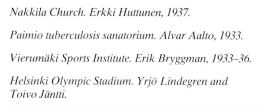

Nakkila Church. Erkki Huttunen, 1937.

Paimio tuberculosis sanatorium. Alvar Aalto, 1933.

Vierumäki Sports Institute. Erik Bryggman, 1933–36.

Helsinki Olympic Stadium. Yrjö Lindegren and Toivo Jäntti.

---

standard units can be combined to produce lively architecture. Most of the buildings were low, narrow strips, but the restaurant, placed higher up on a hillside, was round. Tall, narrow advertising columns added vivid vertical accents to the composition. Advertising graphics took the place of conventional facade design. According to Elina Standertskjöld, these graphics determined the look of the event.

The actual physical breakthrough of Functionalism was delayed by the economic recession of 1930. Early individual buildings of note include Bryggman's Hospits Betel (1929) and Aalto's Turun Sanomat newspaper offices in Turku (1930). On a narrow but deep plot at Kauppiaskatu 1 in the middle of town, Aalto placed the most up-to-date newspaper building in Scandinavia, complete with printing works and editorial offices. In the top storey, the forward-looking client had his own spacious flat with a rooftop terrace. The reinforced concrete frame extends six storeys above ground and two storeys below. For the streetside section, Aalto

applied Le Corbusier's five principles: the house was built on *pilotis*, it had a rooftop garden, each storey had a free floor plan made possible by the frame structure, the building had strip windows to provide maximum light, and the facade composition was free.

The most heated controversies of the time arose in conjunction with church design competitions. No less than 56 architects sent in entries to the Tehtaanpuisto Church competition in 1930. Alarmed by the newfangled ideas, the jury announced a second competition in 1932 with a programme requiring the use of 'traditional church forms'. In the first round, the Turku Modernists had won the three top prizes. A furious newspaper debate ensued: the young architects accused the jury of summoning up the ghosts of history, while the old guard instructed them that a church tower should not look like a factory chimney. The conservatives carried the day, and Lars Sonck's rugged brick church was built.

The first churches in the new style were built in Nakkila (1937) and Kannonkoski (1938). The architect of the large church of Nakkila, on a fine hilltop location above an industrial complex, was Erkki Huttunen (1901–56). The interior is in the shape of a simple rectangle covered by a low pitched roof. The high bell tower is a separate structure rising directly beside the entrance. The form is thoroughly solid and lucid.

P.E. Blomstedt (1900–35) was one of the leading planners and thinkers of the Functionalist breakthrough. In the first competition for Temppeliaukio Church in Töölö back in 1933, he presented a radically modern design, suggesting that the church should be embedded into the rock, with merely the light of the low glass crown seen from the surroundings, which would be left unbuilt. The time was not yet ripe for the idea. Even the church authorities, however, agreed that a modern design was suitable for Kannonkoski, if only because the village had no old ecclesiastical tradition. Blomstedt achieved dynamic form with an interior rising from the altar and pulpit to the entrance. Construction was delayed by the depression: Märta Blomstedt and Matti Lampén signed the final drawings in 1937, two years after the architect's death.

Health care advanced rapidly in Finland in the 1920s and '30s. Besides new methods of treatment, international architectural innovations rapidly met with acceptance. Large sanatoria were built in ozone-rich pine forests for treating the national scourge, tuberculosis. Many of these were impressive monuments to Functionalism, above all Aalto's Paimio Sanatorium, completed in 1933.

The structural frame of the Paimio Sanatorium consists of concrete columns, permitting free floor plans. Aalto spread out the oblong wings in a fan arrangement, using the central entrance section to connect them. He placed the open bedroom wards in a separate southern extension of the patients' wing. As Heinonen points out, the sanatorium provided the ideal assignment for deploying the full Functionalist ideology. The Functionalist demand for air and sunlight corresponded to the theory of TB treatment. In Paimio, Aalto took account of these requirements in all parts of the plan. He worked out every detail in the wards with a view to maximizing the comfort of the patient, who would have to spend long days bedridden. The building is protected under the Building Conservation Act, but the original interiors have only been preserved in a few 'museum rooms'.

The rise in the popularity of physical exercise was an essential ingredient of Finnish life between the wars. Clubs were founded and large-scale building projects were undertaken. The Finnish Sports Institute, founded in 1927, initiated construction of training facilities at Vierumäki. Erik Bryggman won the design competition in 1930. The project was delayed, but when President Kallio inaugurated the institute in 1937, the press ran headlines extolling "the White House of Finnish sports".

The rectangular central section of the Institute's main building is seven storeys high and connected to three lower wings. The entrances and main staircase are placed at the intersections. At the rear, the building rises perpendicu-

The housing area originally built as an Olympic village was designed 1939–40 by Hilding Ekelund and Martti Välikangas.

larly from the edge of the lakeside slope; on the entrance side, the composition of varying height faces a quiet pine forest. Bryggman intended the frame to be cast concrete, but ultimately a more traditional construction method was adopted. Only the bearing columns were cast of concrete, whereas the walls were made of brick, and the strip windows of the plan gave way to equal-sized openings producing a staccato effect.

Helsinki's Olympic Stadium raised Functionalism into a symbol of modern Finland. The winners of the architectural competition were Yrjö Lindegren (1900–52) and Toivo Jäntti (1900–75), who produced a plan of unmatched vigour and lightness. The first construction phase was completed in 1938, but enlargement began immediately, as the 1940 Olympic Games had been awarded to Helsinki. The event was cancelled because of the war, and further extensions were built before the Games were finally held in 1952. The original low basic structure was successively extended. Renovation of the reinforced concrete structures will be necessary in the 1990s, as they have not stood up to the test of time quite as well as expected.

In preparation for the Olympic Games, Helsinki also built its first Functionalist housing district, the Olympic Village, a residential area of high quality built in 1939–40 to plans by Hilding Ekelund and Martti Välikangas. The buildings are simple but varied, and the way they are placed on the sloping site gives rise to especially pleasant courtyards. In the very first modern Finnish suburb, nature had a more significant role than in most international precedents. Ekelund developed small family apartments of unsurpassed flexibility for the area.

A second Functionalist district was built beyond Sibelius Park in Taka-Töölö ('Rear Töölö') to a town plan drawn up by Birger Brunila in 1937. The three-storey houses, designed by architects and master builders, were as simple as possible but carefully scaled. The remainder of the district filled up in the 1930s with large blocks of flats. In places, the houses formed closed blocks fronting the streets, as in the old town plan; elsewhere, open block structures appeared. This massive urban development still awaits closer study: the concept of 'Töölö Functionalism' is familiar to most Finns who take an interest in architecture.

Erkki Huttunen was the architect who took Functionalism to the provincial towns and the countryside. In his work at the building department of the Central Finnish Co-operative Society (SOK) and for the Finnish alcohol monopoly as well as in his private practice, he produced numerous impressive factory and co-operative shop buildings. In Rauma, he built the SOK office and warehouse (1931) and Raumanlinna, the civilian defence corps building (1933), in Oulu another SOK office and warehouse

The SOK offices and warehouse in Oulu, Erkki Huttunen 1938.

(1938), and dozens of clean-lined business buildings throughout Finland. Teppo Jokinen's study of Huttunen's work lists 144 planning assignments in the years 1928–39.

The State artillery factory built the largest Functionalist housing district outside Helsinki in Jyväskylä from 1937 to 1939. The Rautpohja district consisted of two two-storey blocks of flats for officials and twelve for workers, sandwiched between the factory and Rautpohjankatu. The plans were drawn up at the Defence Ministry's building office, which also quickly adopted Functionalism as the style for military barracks. The Rautpohja managers' and officials' housing was designed by Märtha Lilius-Tallroth (1904–), the workers' housing by Airi Seikkala-Viertokangas (1908–60). Anne Mäkinen added a new chapter to the history of Functionalism in Finland with her research on women architects at the Defence Ministry.

Erik Bryggman

The Classicism of the early work of Erik Bryggman (1891–1955) made way for Functionalism without any abrupt transition. His Functionalist masterpieces, the Vierumäki sports institute and the book tower of Turku's Swedish university (Åbo Akademi) library (completed 1935) prove that the essence of architecture is in its proportions, not in stylistic labels. The pure white cube of the book tower gently introduced Functionalism to one of the most demanding building sites in the whole country, next to the mediaeval cathedral and nestling up to the 19th-century wood town.

With the same composure, Bryggman abandoned the strict whiteness of Functionalism in the late 1930s, giving materials a new value. The Sampo Insurance Company headquarters (1938) at the corner of Turku's market square contained the long-lived Lehtinen Café, for which Bryggman designed the interiors.

After the wars, Bryggman contributed to residential planning with Läntinen Rantakatu 21 in Turku (1949–51), a block of flats long held up as an example to be imitated. The free overall plan, roughcast facades and decorative balcony railings were common features in later government-subsidized housing.

In designing summer villas for the Turku surroundings, Bryggman took his ideal of living in harmony with nature furthest. The early Villa Solin, built on a fine seaside plot in Katariinanlaakso, poetically combined receding Classicist touches with Functionalist clarity. Built 1933, the Villa Warén on Ruissalo island was entirely in the new spirit. Its quiet clifftop garden has an ascetic beauty with something like Japanese sensitivity. According to Esa Piiroinen, the Villa

Chapel of the Resurrection, Turku. Erik Bryggman, 1941.

Ekman (1933) in Hirvensalo and the Villa Kaino (1935) in Kakskerta are variations on the Villa Warén.

The Villa Nuuttila, built 1949 in Kuusisto, is the freest of all of Bryggman's works. It is in the form of a twisting chain, and the drama of its cliff site is enhanced by enormous boulders and ancient oak trees. Stairs branch out in every direction both indoors and outside. Window sizes and shapes vary, depending on the room plans and views. Low, pitched roofs and soapstone-faced foundations and terraces reinforce the sense of organic unity with the landscape.

Bryggman's church and chapel designs constitute the most refined contribution to Finnish religious architecture in our century. From his first competition entries in 1919 to the posthumously completed funeral chapels of Honkanummi, Lohja and Lappeenranta, he immersed himself in the aesthetics of church architecture with unequalled enthusiasm. Basing his plans on the aesthetic values of the surroundings, he gave natural light the principal role in his interiors.

The Chapel of the Resurrection in Turku (1938–41) is the mature synthesis of Bryggman's architecture, one of the key works of the post-Functionalist idyll in Europe. Its architecture features slightly oblique angles, gentle, plastic forms and a variety of soft materials. The interior has an irregular barrel vault for a ceiling, and the full length of one wall opens up to a pine forest.

Alvar Aalto

No stylistic epithet quite explains why the architecture of Alvar Aalto (1898–1976) makes such a deep impression. Aalto was a past master in applying international theories and influences. Even in his most militant Functionalist phase, he was never hostile to history or to the caprices of the natural world. Kirmo Mikkola called Aalto a vitalist to whom nothing human was alien.

During the prolonged process of planning Viipuri Library, Aalto accomplished the shift from Classicism to Functionalism. The entry which won him the commission in 1927 resembled Gunnar Asplund's Stockholm City Library in many ways. As it was built in Torkkeli park, Aalto's library became a monument to Functionalism, liberated from all historicist reference, with free interior planning and ingenious lighting arrangements at its artistic core. The purely cubic composition also meant a first step on the road from rectangularity to free form and a new respect for the intrinsic value of natural materials: the ceiling and rear wall of the auditorium have a free, undulating form and a surface consisting of untreated pine battens.

In the Finnish pavilions at the 1937 and 1939 World's Fairs in Paris and New York, Aalto boldly developed the Finnish aesthetic of wood and free form. He offered up to his international public the products of the Finnish wood-

Viipuri City Library.
Alvar Aalto, 1935.

Villa Mairea.
Alvar Aalto, 1939.

processing industry as a visual feast, a symphony of wood.

The Villa Mairea in Noormarkku, designed by Alvar Aalto and Aino Marsio-Aalto (1894–1949) for their friends Harry and Maire Gullichsen in 1938–39, gave the architects an opportunity to experiment freely with new forms and materials. The spacious private house grew into an unconventional, undemonstrative total work of art, a sequence of freely combined spaces merging with the surroundings. Bare wood surfaces, white rendered walls, with glazed tile and soapstone for a few details, the fieldstones of the garden wall; all the various forms and materials combined to produce extraordinary harmony.

Alvar Aalto also initiated a reform in the structure of industrial communities. The terraced house built for the Ahlström company's Kauttua mill in 1937–38 was intended to herald a new kind of housing for workers. His more ambitious plans for Kauttua never materialized, however.

In designing the Sunila pulp mill on a previously undeveloped island near Kotka in 1936, Aalto had the opportunity to put his new principles to the test in designing a whole community. He placed the factory buildings on the island and the housing in a fan arrangement on the mainland, following the lie of the land. Standing high on its cliff foundation, the mill is a sculpturesque monument to labour. Aalto's intention was to make the housing district a modern industrial town by providing its inhabitants with urban amenities combined with an unspoilt setting. He also attempted to break down established class divisions in the placement of the housing: externally, the carefully planned 'chain houses' and row houses did not reveal the status of their occupants in the company.

After the war, Aalto made a major contribution to the field of standard housing. His work for industrial enterprises in the 1930s had provided a solid foundation for this work. Aalto's dream was to make the reconstruction of Finland a kind of international architectural laboratory, the results of which would be valid far beyond the immediate needs of the post-war shortages. Aalto set out to develop standardization, fully aware from the outset of the dangers of its mechanical application. Sigfried Giedion wrote that Aalto was the strongest of the architects who combined standardization with the irrational, making standardization man's servant and not his master.

In the words of Pekka Suhonen, Säynätsalo Town Hall (completed in 1952) "... stands among the pines like a small castle: the impression arises from the tower of the assembly chamber and the firm though friendly reticence of the building, huddling around its enclosed courtyard. The courtyard, which affords glimpses of the surroundings via the staircase and steep,

planted terraces, is raised one storey above ground level. With its intimate atmosphere, the courtyard, which serves as a route to the municipal offices and library, stands in contrast to the monumentality of the exterior architecture. Its very ingredients – glass, metal, strips of white plaster, grass, the fountain and the sensitive forms of Wäinö Aaltonen's Cubist sculpture are like a new melody in counterpoint to the brick surfaces."

Säynätsalo Town Hall opened a fine series of red-brick buildings in Aalto's output, soon continued in nearby Jyväskylä. Construction of the new main building of the Institute of Pedagogics (since 1966 the University of Jyväskylä), began in 1952 on a site near the old seminary. Aalto's plan assembled the fragmentary district into an ordered whole. The assembly hall and administrative centre was built first at the the head of a street which rises to the hilly site from the centre of town. Over the next twenty years, the various faculties sprang up around campus lawns and a sports field.

The centre of Seinäjoki was Aalto's most monumental urban plan to be carried out. The project started when he won the planning competition for the church in 1951, but only really got under way when the church was completed in 1960. Six years later, the lower parish centre building which frames the church was completed. The Town Hall (1962) and public library

(1965) face the church, contrasting the everyday life of the townspeople with the gleaming white religious structure. The paved area between, known as the Citizens' Square, was completed in 1988, framed at the back by the Government Office Building (1968). Nightlife in the centre picked up when the municipal theatre, designed by Aalto in 1969, was finally built 1986–87 under the supervision of Elissa Aalto (1923–). The terracing of the site points up the individuality of sculpturesque forms in Seinäjoki's central buildings; the importance of the Town Hall is underscored by the dark blue glazed tiles used for its walls. The green patina of copper roofs completes the colour scale.

Apart from the architect's own home, a small newsstand built 1951 at Erottaja and the Engineers' Building (1952) were the first buildings designed by Aalto in Helsinki. He won prizes in competitions, but had no major assignments in the capital before the Rautatalo ('Iron House'), which was built on Keskuskatu in 1954. Here Aalto solved the problem of designing a facade for a new structure among older buildings from different periods in a closed block by carefully scaled fenestration. The covered courtyard provided a quiet refuge from one of Helsinki's liveliest streets.

In both the exterior and the interior of the Academic Bookshop (or 'Book Palace'), built 1969, Alvar and Elissa Aalto further developed

Seinäjoki town centre, designed by Alvar Aalto. Church, 1960; parish centre, 1966; town hall, 1962; library, 1965.

Säynätsalo Town Hall. Alvar Aalto, 1952.

House of Culture, Helsinki. Alvar Aalto, 1958.

the themes of the Rautatalo. The two buildings harmoniously flank a red-brick business building designed by Eliel Saarinen in the early 1920s.

The National Pensions Institute headquarters, built 1952–56, is the most spectacular building in the district of Taka-Töölö. The rhythmic composition links the complex on every side to the surrounding urban structure. The Mannerheimintie facade, partly in granite, is the building's most monumental element; the horizontally descending red-brick facade at the back the gentlest.

The House of Culture on Sturenkatu, built 1955–58, consists of two parts. The curving, sculpturesque red-brick walls of the concert hall proclaim the public nature of this section far and wide. The more pedestrian five-storey office wing, with its darkening copper facade, withdraws shyly from the streetline. The complex is held together by a streetside canopy and a low, connecting wing at the back of the plot. The concert hall is still one of Helsinki's best.

The main building of the Helsinki University of Technology in Otaniemi (1955–64) is based on the Otaniemi town plan, which Aalto drew up as early as 1949. With its high, fan-shaped auditorium, placed at the crossing of old tree-lined lanes, the main building towers above the spacious campus and the red-brick grid formed by the library, administrative offices and various faculties. Only the architecture department has

white marble in its facades. The broad lawn meets the main auditorium at the paved piazza of an amphitheatre.

Of Aalto's churches, Vuoksenniska Church, built 1956–58, is a small but remarkably monumental sculptural experience, with its soft play of light on freely curving wall surfaces. Leonardo Mosso holds Vuoksenniska Church to be the first masterpiece of Aalto's second white period: "the interior, moving and ever-growing in the tripartite volume of the church, is like a musical instrument for the voice and soul".

From 1961 to 1972, Aalto worked on a monumental vision for the centre of Helsinki, consisting of a large, fan-shaped, terraced square and a series of cultural buildings, set along the west shore of Töölö Bay like a string of pearls. The only fragment of the plan to be carried out consisted of the Finlandia Hall (1971) and its congress wing (1975), the splendid culmination of Aalto's white period. The white Carrara marble used for the facades adds a lyrical glow to the complex structure. Viewed from Mannerheimintie, the Finlandia Hall provides a meandering backdrop to the park, while the more straightforward and massively sculptural east facade dominates the Helsinki skyline from afar. The building is protected under the Building Conservation Act, but the city has long postponed the decision to replace the inferior marble used for the facades.

Helsinki University of Technology main building, Otaniemi. Alvar Aalto, 1964.

Postwar reconstruction

After the Second World War, the residents of Karelia had to leave their homes and resettle in the west. Over 400,000 people left: 120,000 homes were destroyed or abandoned in territory ceded to the Soviet Union. This was about one-tenth of all Finnish homes. These Karelian Finns were resettled more quickly and permanently – within five or six years – than refugees in other European countries. With the intention of providing for the refugees living conditions similar to those they had left behind, the reconstruction programme initially focused on rural areas. Nearly 150,000 new farmsteads were established under the Land Acquisition Act.

The government tackled the housing shortage in towns in 1949 by establishing the 'Arava system', which consisted of State-subsidized loans for housing construction. Production was intense until the late 1950s: for the housing construction business, the reconstruction period lasted until 1956 or 1958. This period has sometimes been called the Age of Heroic Materialism. Anneli Juntto gave a concise explanation of the term: "People believed in progress and

longed for material security. All social strata worked together for a common goal. The criteria of social policy and housing development were still largely political rather than economic, as were the keeping of social peace and the safeguarding of legitimacy. The aim was to make up 'for the loss of just rights', to make amends to the war veterans, to 'pay off the debt of honour'." Opening the Nordic Building Congress in 1955, Prime Minister Urho Kekkonen proudly stated that Finland had built almost 250,000 new homes since the war.

Finland never resorted to building temporary emergency housing. Instead, the goal was a lasting reform of the principles of planning. Ministries and a plethora of non-profit associations started developing standard plans to help builders do their work as quickly, safely and well as possible. The authorities could rely on private initiative in actual construction. The Ministry of Social Affairs and the Ministry of Agriculture arranged a planning competition for standard housing, the results of which were published as early as 1940 in "A Selection of Standard Plans for Small Rural Houses".

The most common type of house was very uniform. It was in the shape of a cube, with a frame built of logs or boards, a high foundation and one residential storey proper. Under the pitched roof was a high attic which could be converted into bedrooms. The ground plan was

Standard houses from the reconstruction years, Pieksämäki.

virtually square, and a stove was placed in the centre, the most economical solution to the problem of heating. The smaller type houses had only a living-room-cum-kitchen and a bedroom on the main floor. The larger ones had a kitchen, bedroom and living room forming a continuum with the hall. In front of the hall was a closed but unheated porch.

The signature of the individual architect can hardly be detected in the standard house. In her analysis of the standard house as a cultural system manifesting and regulating home life, Kirsi Saarikangas showed what a narrow role division its plan was based on. The home was the housewife's realm in which the father merely had a visitor's role. This was the basic social unit of the reconstruction period, the family which was expected to produce lots of children.

In 1942 the Finnish Association of Architects set up a reconstruction office. Under the leadership of Viljo Revell (1910–64), the office produced standard plans and gave planning assistance. Its planners included Aulis Blomstedt (1906–79), Kaj Englund (1905–76), Aarne Hytönen (1901–72), Yrjö Lindegren, Olli Pöyry (1924–73) and Erkki Koiso-Kanttila (1914–). Standardization led to the introduction of a building information file in 1943; the 'RT cards' produced under this system were the most powerful influence on the development of Finnish building standards.

In addition to owner-built houses, prefabricated small houses were also developed. Puutalo Oy was founded in 1940 as a joint sales organization for twenty wooden house factories. According to Pekka Korvenmaa, the designers of factory-made houses concentrated on basic types of flexible size, seeking to profit from the experiences of the U.S. house industry. According to Saarikangas, the most popular Puutalo model was 'Syväaho', designed by Jorma Järvi (1908–62) and Erik Lindroos (1906–80), which was closest to the one-and-a-half storey standard house plan. Demand for the prefabricated houses was not very high: only 105 houses were sold in 1940.

Alvar Aalto organized, wrote and lectured about standard housing, and drafted plans. Construction of the war veterans' village in Tampere's Nekala district began as a voluntary community project during the hiatus in the war in 1941. Aalto designed the single-storey wooden houses, the parts for which were prefabricated by the Ahlström company's Varkaus house factory. Construction continued during the Continuation War, and the fourteen two-family houses were completed in autumn 1943. With their horizontal weatherboarding and large porches, Aalto's houses differed from later types.

Among the first suburbs of single-family homes were those in which 2,000 prefabricated wooden houses donated by Sweden were erected. The houses were designed in Finland to

Swedish standards: for example, the low 'Swedish houses' of two or three rooms in Helsinki's Pirkkola district were designed by Lauri Pajamies (1899–1959).

Erik Bryggman was the planner of the Pansio housing district in Turku, built 1946–47 for the shipbuilding company Laivateollisuus Oy. Using light fences to mark off family gardens, he developed a lively, rhythmic plan for an area of ascetic standard wooden houses in the shadow of giant oak trees. Unfortunately, most of these trees were cut down during construction.

Along with resettlement farms, groups of ordinary type houses constitute the finest postwar monument to Finnish endurance. They were erected on the fringes of cities and towns throughout the country. Not much attention was given to town planning: large plots of equal size were laid out along a few straight or curving streets, and a limit was set on how much of the plot could be covered by buildings. The remaining land was intended to be used as an orchard, garden and vegetable patch to provide sustenance and pleasure to the family. Large trees, dense bushes and colourful perennials lend these houses such charm that few can understand why similar areas were heedlessly demolished only twenty years ago to make way for new row houses. A comparison with photographs from the early '50s reveals how different they looked then.

The Finnish forest town

Otto-I. Meurman (1890–) was appointed Finland's first professor of town planning in 1940. He published his ideas in a book entitled *The Theory of Town Planning* in 1947. In Meurman's urban ideal, nature takes precedence over man's works; roads and buildings tactfully blend with natural forms. Meurman illustrated his views on urban planning with a diagram in the shape of a tree, emphasizing his integral organic philosophy. One detects the influence of Lewis Mumford's *Culture of Cities*, published in Finnish translation in 1949.

Meurman's key planning principle is decentralization. 'Townships' are separated from one another by unbuilt forests, farmland or parks. A township comprises a business centre, industrial areas, warehouses and traffic areas – separated from each other and from housing areas by green belts – as well as administrative, educational and cultural facilities, institutional services and a shopping centre. Townships are divided into smaller, separate neighbourhoods, which are served by a local shop, school, post office and meeting facility, with a smattering of industrial workshops. The size of a neighbourhood is determined mainly on the basis of school district divisions: Meurman suggested 6,000 as an ideal figure. A neighbourhood is further divided into housing cells; in addition to housing, these cells

Chain houses on
Menninkäisentie,
Aulis Blomstedt
1954.

Modern prefabricated
construction
techniques were tried
out in the Kontiontie
row houses. Kaija
and Heikki Siren,
1954.

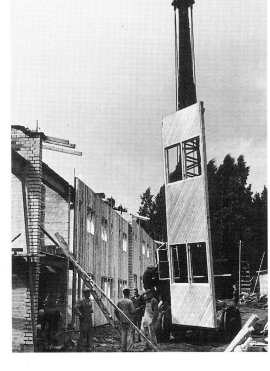

Tapiola garden
town, early 1960s.

Jorma Järvi planned this area of low single-family homes near the centre of Tapiola.

contain a nursery school, cafeteria, playrooms and hobby rooms, garage, laundry and heating plant for approximately 100 people.

Meurman's principles were straightforwardly pragmatic. He thought a good town could be built by organizing basic everyday needs in a sensible way. His philosophy was later criticized mainly for its negative attitude to densely-built urban centres.

The term 'forest town' was invented in the 1960s as a criticism of Meurman's planning ideas; at the same time, however, it summed up the positive qualities of the new urban vision. Meurman adapted the inherited wisdom of rural building to urban development. He pondered the terrain and microclimate of every plot with an earnestness unthinkable in large-scale urban utopias. Now that the technoutopia has collapsed and large-scale planning seems increasingly frightening to us, Meurman's forest town is again beginning to look like a possible way to achieve ecologically sustainable progress.

The most polemically anti-urban document of the Finnish forest town ideology was the pamphlet "Do Our Children Need Homes or Barracks?", written by Heikki von Hertzen, head of the Finnish Population and Family Welfare Federation, and published 1946.

Von Hertzen declared that Helsinki held "the world record in building barracks". He thought the city districts built in the 1920s a pure

mistake: closed block structure and straight streets could not provide a life worth living. In vividly metaphorical language, the booklet blamed the bad habits of city youth on the urban environment. A healthy lifestyle could only be fostered amid leafy groves and green meadows and on the beaches. As his models for the built environment, von Hertzen presented several housing areas built in Sweden in the 1940s. Wood Käpylä was the only Finnish example that passed the test.

Von Hertzen set up Asuntosäätiö, a non-profit housing foundation, to build the Tapiola garden town in Espoo. The town plan for land purchased from Hagalund Manor was drawn up under Meurman's direction according to the principles of his 'town planning theory'. Each neighbourhood had its own day-care centre and school; the administration, the church, culture and commerce each had a plot in the district centre at the crossing of the major thoroughfares. The residential plots were of considerable depth, with a planted forecourt between the curving streets and the buildings. The former manorial fields were turned into informal outdoor leisure areas.

Originally, about one half of the dwellings were to be in blocks of flats, the remainder were to consist of single-family homes and row houses. Meurman considered the latter especially suitable for low-income families. With some few

The Cultural Centre, designed by Arto Sipinen (1989), completed the centre of Tapiola, planned by Aarne Ervi from 1954 on.

exceptions, the apartment houses were to be no higher than three storeys. The details of the plan were left to the architects.

In spring 1952, Aulis Blomstedt, Aarne Ervi (1910–77), Viljo Revell and Markus Tavio (1911–78) started working together with Meurman on the first stage of the plan, Tapiola's eastern neighbourhood. Owing to the housing shortage, the number and size of apartment houses had to be increased, and Meurman resigned from the project in protest.

Riitta Hurme has studied the way that detailed planning advanced only slightly ahead of construction. The secret of the area's best features may lie in this flexibility. The blending of terrain and architecture was extremely fine, and garden plans were given high priority. The landscape architect Carl-Johan Gottberg recalls that before final approval of house plans, their corners and floor heights, and even the height of the eaves, were marked on the site.

Asunto Oy Mäntytorni, an eleven-storey tower block designed by Ervi and comprising some 60 studio flats, a café and offices, was built 1954 in the centre of Tapiola's eastern neighbourhood. The slip casting method was used for making the frame. A low wing building at the foot of the tower contained a cinema. On two sides of the adjacent street, Menninkäisentie, Blomstedt designed a harmonious group of three chain houses and three apartment blocks,

with alternating red brick and white plaster surfaces accentuated by window frames sporting the Bauhaus colours yellow, red and blue.

Technical experimentation was part of the Tapiola programme. Ervi and Revell made the boldest use of prefabrication techniques. One of Revell's two blocks of flats on Mäntyviita had prefabricated bearing structures, and its apartments had American-type bar counter kitchens. The house was nicknamed 'the tractor factory', and the small kitchens met with disapproval. The facades of the Kaskenkaatajantie blocks of flats were more elegant. Revell's sculpturesque tower blocks built on Tapiola's highest outcrops in 1959–61 became a landmark that even air travellers can identify.

Markus Tavio designed 'The Five', an attractive group of five point blocks, leaving the most scenic part of the forested hill between the houses as a sheltered courtyard. One year later, he designed another group of four apartment blocks at Otsonkallio on the same principle.

Kaija Siren (1920–) and Heikki Siren (1918–) designed the groups of row houses on Kontiontie and Kimmeltie (built 1955) with prefabricated facade units made of wood. The Sirens later drew up plans for a variety of row houses and apartment blocks in Tapiola, managing to produce strikingly flexible apartment plans despite the strict financial limitations. In the adjacent district of Otaniemi, their chapel (1957) showed

Maunula housing area, designed by Hilding Ekelund in the 1950s.

that ascetic forms and unassuming brick and wood structures suffice to establish an atmosphere of utter sanctity. The altarpiece of this forest chapel is nature: the minuscule monument sums up the pantheism of the Finns.

In the Tapiola Coeducational School (1960), Jorma Järvi produced a new, low school type, with long, narrow wings lightly spaced out among the pines and accentuated by hexagonal pavilions. The Aarnivalkea bungalow homes, designed by Järvi and built 1956-58, form an intimate group of houses quite near the centre. These low single-family homes seem to reflect the strong influence of American architecture on the shaping of the new towns. The one-and-a-half-storey house type was not in favour in new suburbs like Tapiola. In the network of apartment blocks and row houses, bungalows provided a distinctive, earthy touch of their own.

Aarne Ervi won the 1954 planning competition for the centre of Tapiola. His plan turned the former gravel pit into a central pool beside the multistorey Keskustorni (Central Tower). An elegant geometry of proportions accompanies the building's airy rise, which culminates in a 'lighthouse' visible from afar. Shops were placed in a low bazaar at the foot of the tower. Ervi insisted on keeping the garden town a pleasant place for pedestrians. The consumerism of a later age, however, has swallowed up the original small shops, replacing them with massive department stores and supermarkets. Although pedestrian and automobile traffic were separated when the centre was enlarged, the quiet life of the old garden town barely survives in Ervi's small Tapiontori square.

Of Tapiola's later buildings, only the devoutly introverted church (1965) by Aarno Ruusuvuori (1925–1992) and its extension completed in 1993, and Arto Sipinen's rhythmic Cultural Centre (1989) pay tribute to the optimistic spirit of the original plan.

Among Helsinki's new suburbs, Herttoniemi, Maunula, Etelä-Haaga and Roihuvuori come closest to the Tapiola model. Hilding Ekelund drew up the plan for a residential area built 1951–56 by the City of Helsinki Housing Production Committee on a scenic hillside site in Maunula. The first stage of the project consisted of 22 row houses on the lower reaches of the slope. The apartments were terraced on three levels, the lowest having a direct ground-level entrance without intervening stairs. Angular 'point' blocks higher up underscore the sculptural quality of the setting; behind them, narrow 'lamella' blocks follow the terrain contours. Red brick and light rendering alternate in the facades. The overall effect is lively and the courtyards pleasant.

Viljo Revell and Keijo Petäjä (1919–88) used the same materials for their 'folk homes' in Maunula. Ornamental cast balcony railings add

Helsinki School of Economics. Hugo Harmia and Woldemar Baeckman, 1950.

a distinctive trim to the group of fifteen houses. The neighbourhood has its own day-care centre and a service building which originally contained sauna baths, a laundry, workrooms and small shops.

The rocky outcrops of Herttoniemi were also propitious ground for development. The tallest buildings were placed as prominent accents high on the site, with row houses lower down on the slopes.

Master planning, aimed at bringing urban growth under control, only got under way at the time that the first suburbs were built, in 1953 to be precise. An outline plan completed in 1960 proposed a ring of suburbs, with housing for from 5,000 to 10,000 inhabitants, encircling the city core and connected to it by rail.

Technological advances

The postwar shortage of materials kept advances in building technology in check for many years. Experiments in new housing areas tended to indicate that prefabricated units neither speeded up construction nor reduced its cost; there was labour aplenty.

The availability of skilled labour sometimes led to considerable use of decoration in public buildings. Lastenlinna, the Helsinki children's hospital, was designed by Elsi Borg and com-

pleted in 1947 with the collaboration of many artists. Sakari Tohka designed the sculptures of the window posts, and the facades were blanketed with decoration. The rich architecture of the Helsinki School of Economics (1950) on Runeberginkatu, designed by Hugo Harmia (1907–52) and Woldemar Baeckman (1911–), was complemented by Michail Schilkin's ceramic relief depicting economic prosperity.

After the war, architects gradually returned to the Functionalist dream of pure forms arising from building technology. Two milestones were the Teollisuuskeskus building at Eteläranta in Helsinki, better known as the Palace, designed by Keijo Petäjä and completed in 1952 (the year of the Helsinki Olympics) and Porthania, the Helsinki University faculty building, designed by Aarne Ervi and completed in 1957 as the first prefabricated public building in Finland. Both had idiosyncratic but thoroughly coherent designs perfectly adapted to the scale of their surroundings.

Factories and power stations constituted the most direct continuation of Functionalism. The book "Finnish Industrial Architecture", edited by Viljo Revell and published in 1952, presented some impressive industrial environments. The City of Helsinki electricity works in Salmisaari was just being completed to plans by Hilding Ekelund, the giant power plant of Imatra, by K.S. and Oiva Kallio, was already on line. The

Teollisuuskeskus Building ('Palace'). Viljo Revell and Keijo Petäjä, 1952.

Porthania. Aarne Ervi, 1957.

---

taming of the Oulujoki rapids was under way; the Pyhäkoski power plant had been completed in 1949; the Jylhämä plant one year later; and the Pälli and Nuojua plants were under construction. All projects were planned by Aarne Ervi and included housing for workforce.

The triumph of prefabricated concrete in housing construction began in the early 1960s. The largest construction companies started up concentrated production of large prefabricated concrete blocks. Full-scale prefabrication was used for the first time in the southwest part of Helsinki's Pihlajamäki district (1962–65). Lauri Silvennoinen (1921–69) designed the houses to a town plan by Olli Kivinen (1921–). For Silvennoinen, prefab was an art form. Horizontal lamella houses and bold tower blocks stand like a sculptural group on the rocky hilltop site.

The catalogue compiled by Silvennoinen for the 'PRE-FAB' exhibition arranged by the Museum of Finnish Architecture in 1966 contained a poem which showed that the dreams of the 1930s were still alive: "PRE-FAB / an exhibition, pro machine, / as the host of people mutilated, / jammed in machines, grows… / and yet /

the killer is man – / to control a machine you need culture, / love thy neighbour / even when thou buildest."

The most powerful poet of the austere Modernism of the 1960s was Aarno Ruusuvuori. In the churches of Hyvinkää (1961), Huutoniemi in Vaasa (1964) and Tapiola (1965/1993), he demonstrated the aesthetic potential of concrete. The uncompromising minimalism of his architecture stresses the ethical commitment of the Protestant religion and the plain, down-to-earth quality of the national church – not everyone has been pleased with this unembellished interpretation. In the same spirit, Pekka Pitkänen (1927–) made expressive use of concrete in the Chapel of the Holy Cross in Turku (1967), which envelops the sweeping landscape in a lyrical embrace.

Ruusuvuori and his pupils Kristian Gullichsen (1932–), Kirmo Mikkola (1934–1986) and Juhani Pallasmaa (1936–) developed the planning of small houses in the spirit of Mies van der Rohe's aesthetics of frugality, designing both individual summer villas and system housing intended for serial manufacture. The idea of the industrial holiday home system designed for the Ahlström company in 1969 by Gullichsen and Pallasmaa, with the engineer Eero Paloheimo (1936–) responsible for the structures, was that all building parts could be prefabricated: actual construction would thus consist merely of mounting the columns, beams and frame and

The sculpturesque silhouette of Pihlajamäki. Lauri Silvennoinen, 1965.

Hyvinkää Church. Aarno Ruusuvuori, 1961.

Experimental house of the Moduli 225 system. Gullichsen holiday home, Nuuksio. Kristian Gullichsen and Juhani Pallasmaa, 1970.

Kortepohja row houses, Jyväskylä.
Bengt Lundsten, 1969.

Olari housing blocks, Espoo. Simo Järvinen and Eero
Valjakka, 1973.

Espoo's Kivenlahti district. Town plan by Bror
Söderman; 'Amfi' houses by Heikki Koskelo and
Simo Järvinen, 1986; 'Sea Tower' by Järvinen, 1990.

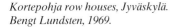

wall units. In this system, named Moduli, Gullichsen and Pallasmaa carried on with the application of Japanese modular wood construction where the studies of Le Corbusier and Aulis Blomstedt had left off. This timelessly beautiful architecture was carried out only in a handful of pilot buildings erected between 1970 and 1974.

Lightweight prefabricated units proved their mettle in the construction of churches for the new suburbs. Vuosaari Church, designed by Ola Laiho (1934–) and Bengt-Vilhelm Levón (1935–), was erected on its rocky site in 1969 without any excavation. Consisting of plywood-faced units on a steel frame, both inside and out the building is more conducive to devout thoughts than many a pompously conventional church.

The compact town

The Finnish rural population began to move to the towns in the 1960s, and migration to Uusi-

maa disrupted the geographical balance of the population. Constant housing shortages induced Helsinki, Espoo and Vantaa to plan ever larger suburbs. In 1959, new building legislation gave local authorities a monopoly on planning within their jurisdiction. Increasing speculative building and the unwillingness of local authorities to purchase land, however, soon wrested control of the booming building trade from the planners.

Helsinki built large housing areas such as Kontula and Myllypuro in the 1960s. Town planning shifted from a respect for terrain contours to a new predominance of the grid. Prefabrication was developed solely with a view to reducing construction costs. Buildings were larger than ever and increasingly monotonous.

The town planning competition for the Kortepohja district of Jyväskylä in 1964 marked the demise of the forest town ideology. The winner Bengt Lundsten (1928–) proposed a plan based on a main axis splitting the area in two, with apartment houses and small houses grouped into square blocks on either side. The block courtyards had a small park at the centre followed by a sequence of spaces increasing in privacy as they approached the individual homes. Vehicular and pedestrian traffic were separated. Of the original plan, only an area of row houses was built (1968–69), acquiring an unusually cheerful look from the rhythmic composition and warm colours of the prefabri-

cated wood units used for the external walls.

The 'Finland Builds' exhibition of 1970 was a major presentation of community planning and the first such event to deal with nature and landscape conservation. Together with Kortepohja, Espoo's Olari district, planned by Simo Järvinen (1938–) and Eero Valjakka (1937–), represented the new compact town at the exhibition. The grid plan, carefully scaled to Olari's rocky terrain, and the aesthetically considered prefabrication techniques used by the architects for the apartment blocks combined to produce the best residential environment of the period.

Among the most ambitious plans of these years were the interim town plan for Vantaa's Koivukylä district, where Pentti Riihelä (1928–), Jaakko Salonen (1934–) and Arno Savela (1935–) proposed to build a rail commuter suburb for from 40,000 to 60,000 inhabitants, and the Pasila town plan, drawn up by the Helsinki City Planning Department under Reijo Jallinoja (1941–) and Paavo Perkkiö (1937–) with the aim of shifting the construction of new workplaces to a new sub-centre. The enormous scale of the plans proved too optimistic: builders concentrated on minimizing costs. In Itä-Pasila (East Pasila), practice showed that the idea of improving pedestrian safety by placing walkways on decks above the motor traffic works only in theory.

The theoretical objective of efficiency also introduced oversize elements into old city dis-

tricts. Viljo Revell designed the massive City block across the street from the Helsinki Railway Station, a colossal central block on Vaasa's market square and the angular KOP building at the corner of Turku's market square. These megablocks, built with robust prefabrication techniques, were completely out of proportion in their rich historical settings. The contrast in scale and form still grates.

Average small-town development in the 1960s and '70s produced unappealing results. Convinced that growth would continue, towns produced new, compact apartment block plans for their old centres. A handful of plots or blocks were built to such plans here and there, often using clumsy prefabrication techniques. The old, coherent wood towns were razed, either entirely or in part. Reunifying the chaotic towns is one of the grand challenges of future builders; the increased sense of history among young architects gives hope that this can be done eventually. Interdisciplinary urban studies are also providing a new foundation for future planning.

The philosophy of the compact town entered a new phase in the 1970s. The Asuntosäätiö foundation started building a densely-built seaside suburb in Espoo's Kivenlahti to a plan by Bror Söderman (1934–). The Amfi houses, a group soaring up from the very shoreline (1982–86, by Heikki Koskelo and Simo Järvinen) and the tall Sea Tower (Järvinen 1990) bring the

Housing at the tip of Katajanokka peninsula, viewed from the sea.

The differences between East and West Pasila show how rapidly the principles of urban development changed in Finland.

---

network of scenically rectangular blocks into focus. Itäkeskus, a large housing and business district was built as a new centre for Helsinki's eastern suburbs. The red-brick housing is straightforward. In the first shopping centre (1984) and the tall Maamerkki (Landmark) office building (1987), Erkki Kairamo (1936–) made elegant use of an emphatically technological architectural idiom. The red-brick multipurpose centre and St. Matthew's Church, designed by Björn Krogius (1940–) and Veli-Pekka Tuominen (1940–), flank a plaza dominated by Hannu Sirén's blue sculpture 'Stoa', standing in quiet contrast to the shopping centre's commercial bustle across the street.

A town planning competition for the Katajanokka harbour district in 1972 resulted in victory for Vilhelm Helander (1941–), Pekka Pakkala (1943–) and Mikael Sundman (1947–), whose entry reintroduced the closed block into the centre of Helsinki. The compact housing district was built between 1977 and 1986, with a granite embankment in the best tradition of

Helsinki's shoreline development and a spacious block structure with large courtyards tying in with traditional local building practice.

Länsi-Pasila (West Pasila), built across the main railway line from its heavily criticized eastern counterpart from 1979 on, shows how easily the basic idea of the compact town could be turned into almost its exact antithesis. Länsi-Pasila is divided into a zone of large public buildings and business offices between the railway and Keskuspuisto park and an area of large but polished housing blocks marked off by curving streets. The shifts between forms and materials within the area are pleasantly restrained. The light-coloured blocks at the north end, designed by Jan Söderlund (1983), are grouped around Rahakamarintori square. The most striking business building fronting the railway is Ilmo Valjakka's cheerfully Post-Modern Kuvalehti Building (1987); Juha Leiviskä's large Auroranlinna (1985) forms a splendid, sculptural south wall to the entire district.

Raili and Reima Pietilä

A powerful counterforce to the prevailing rectangular system of coordinates was quick to arise. Raili (1926–) and Reima Pietilä (1923–93) won the architectural competition for Tapiola's Suvikumpu housing area in 1962 with a plan

deriving its leitmotifs from landscape forms. Built from 1967 to 1982, Suvikumpu became Finland's most purely sculptural exercise in apartment house design. The buildings, varying in height, form rhythmically varied chains of light and dark surfaces merging with the forest.

With Dipoli, the University of Technology student union building in Otaniemi, the Pietiläs demonstrated the potential for free form inherent in concrete. The assembly hall and meeting rooms housed in irregular segments rising from great slabs of rock meet a chequerboard pattern of offices within the building. The bold interior architecture has been regrettably tamed with later additions of conventional furnishing elements and materials. In Tampere's Kaleva Church, which dates from the same period as Dipoli, high, concave concrete blocks give rise to a free-form ground plan sometimes interpreted as the early Christian symbol of the fish. Standing high up on a hill, the church provides a solemn focus to the modest but dignified postwar residential areas around it.

In the 1970s, the architectural duo tackled Tampere's disjointed and overbuilt Hervanta district and – to use Reima Pietilä's own phrase – girded it up with a red belt, consisting of an expressive ensemble of ecclesiastical, municipal and commercial facilities. The use of red brick for facades is a link between the very different buildings: the church is peacefully introverted,

whereas the powerful arch forms of the shopping mall withstand even the hard glare of advertising lights. The new Tampere City Library (1985), built on the edge of Hämeenpuisto park, has been nicknamed 'The Capercaillie' because of its plan view.

From 1973 to 1979 Reima Pietilä worked as professor of Oulu University, influencing the approach of a whole generation of architects. His literary and visually complex architectural philosophy awakened a new self-confidence in the north, giving rise to a 'School of Oulu', which adopted a critical attitude to the southern mainstream.

The essence of Pietilä's architecture has been captured best by Roger Connah in his epic book *Writing Architecture*.

Pluralistic prosperity

Favourable economic development accompanied the building of Finland for a long period which lasted until the early 1990s. The consistent Modernism of the Helsinki University of Technology, named the 'Cool Helsinki School' by the British critic Peter Davey, was opposed by the Oulu masters, who called themselves regionalists. Citizens accused architects of spoiling the environment with their concrete monstrosities, but nowhere could sponsors for in situ building

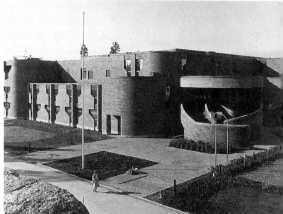

Kaleva Church (1966) by Reima and Raili Pietilä, interior. Photo: Raili Pietilä.

Hervanta parish and recreation centre. Raili and Reima Pietilä, 1979.

be found, although architects daydreamed about them in their seminars. The expert and the man of the street have been unable to reach any kind of consensus about what really goes to make quality in the built environment.

As the country prospered, single-family houses began to take over from apartment blocks in housing construction. House architecture tends to point up the tension between the coherent environment and pronounced individuality. The Finn will not readily submit to instructions when building his own house. The best overall environments have emerged as a result of comprehensive town planning and housing design – there are plenty of examples of the jumble resulting from unbridled individual dreams all around the country. The house industry has fostered the confusion, displaying a growing range of readymade houses to the bewildered public at summer housing fairs over the past few decades. These designs are about as far removed as can be from the universality and durability essential to the original idea of the standard house. In the hustle and bustle of the fairs, serious architectural efforts have tended to be obscured by kitsch.

Helsinki and Espoo show many examples of controlled low-rise development, both in entirely new districts and in additions to old suburbs. In designing these, many architects have developed prefabricated construction in a more flexible direction, giving rise to coherent ensembles which seem to fulfil the disparate requirements of individuality and universality.

For the last decade or more, foreign observers have marvelled that the steady progress of Finnish architecture has been undisturbed by Post-Modern fads. Their views have been based on the most ambitious achievements of Finnish architecture; they have rarely ventured into suburban alleyways. It is interesting, however, that even those Finns who criticized the cool Modernism of Helsinki as outdated never publicly rallied under the banner of Post-Modernism in the 1980s. The great 'Modern Project' is still part of Finland's cultural heritage: controversy has always concentrated on the question of whose 'Modern' is best.

The most renowned building of the Oulu School was Oulunsalo Town Hall, designed by the office of Reijo Niskasaari (1945–88), Kari Niskasaari (1957–), Kaarlo Viljanen (1952–), Ilpo Väisänen (1950–) and Jorma Öhman. The architects explained their red-brick castle in the plains in regionalist terms: they wished to fur-

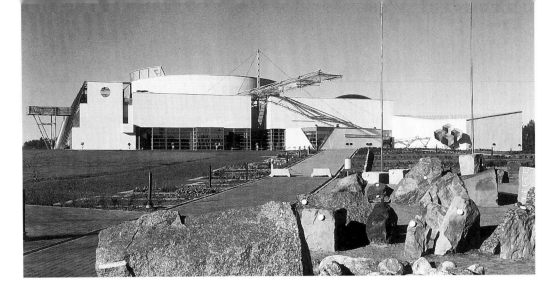

Heureka science centre, Vantaa. Mikko Heikkinen, Markku Komonen, 1988.

Oulunsalo Town Hall. Kari and Reijo Niskasaari, Ilpo Väisänen, Kaarlo Viljanen and Jorma Öhman, 1983.

Tilkankatu 7, block of flats in Pikku-Huopalahti, Helsinki. Reijo Jallinoja, 1993.

Rovaniemi Art Museum. Juhani Pallasmaa, 1986.

nish the sparsely-settled community with a monument which would become part of local history. The most highly acclaimed of the Oulu architects was Heikki Taskinen (1940–92): in his sturdy, meticulously designed red-brick schools, he provided pleasant recreational facilities for students and took special care to create a stimulating classroom environment. The Linnanmaa teacher training primary school was completed in 1981, the Oulu teacher training middle and senior secondary school in 1984 and the Oulunsalo school in 1985.

The Helsinki district of Pikku Huopalahti, started in the late 1980s, gradually developed into a cornucopia of Finnish Post-Modernism. The motley forms, materials and colours are at odds with every Finnish tradition. However, the well-tended outdoor spaces and especially the shoreline give reason to expect that growing verdure will eventually soften the area into just another moderate curiosity in the Finnish capital's rich urban network.

The Modern tradition

A frequently suggested explanation for the strength of Modernism in Finland is that Finns never grew up in the midst of varied historical architecture. All peoples develop their special limitations and strengths within their own cul-

ture. Every architect grows up into a tradition, which he either accepts or rebels against, but he can never break free from his roots. In a country where only one building in eight is over sixty years old, Modernism is a tradition.

In his book *Modern Architecture. A Critical History*, Kenneth Frampton selected Finland's architecture in the 1980s as an example of one of the few enduring achievements in a chaotic world. According to Frampton, Finns added to their respect for the straightforward fundamental principles of Modernism an interdisciplinary reflective practice taking the individual requirements of each planning assignment into account. In a similar spirit, William J.R. Curtis wrote that Finnish architects had always engaged in a comfortable dialogue with the rest of the world. "The best Finnish work of the 1980s seems to be nourished from within as well as without: it is resilient enough to take what it needs from the international arena and open enough not to get trapped in a provincial corner. Geographical remoteness may have insured a certain distance from the flight paths of international fashion, but this does not seem to have diminished the curiosity of the young for what goes on in California, Paris or Portugal, any more than distance stopped an earlier generation from finding out about France, Holland and Germany."

Public opinion at home tends to look back on the architecture of the '80s as too many bank

Ararat Lodge, Juva.
Georg Grotenfelt,
1986.

offices, oversize shopping centres and prefabricated house packages of dubious quality. Foreign authorities focus on the many breathtakingly beautiful churches, versatile cultural centres and libraries built in Finland, and the fact that municipal offices, old people's homes, suburban multipurpose centres, day-care centres, social housing and even large industrial complexes were turned into authentic, artistic architecture.

Pekka Helin (1945–) and Tuomo Siitonen (1946–) designed numerous residential buildings as well as public buildings such as the UKK Institute in Tampere (1984), the multipurpose centre with indoor swimming pool in Hollola (1986) and the Jyväskylä air terminal (1988), all in a fresh, expressive modern idiom. The inventive day-care centres and high-quality planning in the difficult field of social housing of Kari Järvinen (1940–) and Timo Airas (1947–) earned them a government award in 1986. Sofianlehdonkatu 10 (1988) in Helsinki extends the proud 1920s streetscape of Mäkelänkatu in the form of a rock fortress. The sheltered inner courtyard is a modern version of the old large courtyard block. All of the apartments overlook the courtyard, which contains the complex's own day-care centre.

The Heureka science centre (1988) by Mikko Heikkinen (1949–) and Markku Komonen (1945–) is a building of cosmic dimensions, a passionate love affair between technology and nature. Rovaniemi air terminal (1992) successfully links the speed of flight with the static landscape.

In the Stockmann department store extension (1989), Kristian Gullichsen succeeded in unifying a complex historical townscape with – in his own words – "a translucent architecture of light containing the contextualism and ambiguity favoured by our era". His Poleeni Cultural Centre in Pieksämäki (1989) brings together the small-scale Functionalism and charming lakeshore site of the small railway junction in a long, wall-like mass with an exterior arousing a variety of associations which strengthen the *genius loci* and emphasize the importance of culture.

Many prominent old buildings in the centre of Helsinki have been revitalized by successful restoration. The restoration and enlargement of the Ateneum Art Museum under Ola Laiho set a fine example, turning the Finnish National Gallery into a living centre of visual arts.

By minimalist architectural and sculptural means, Juhani Pallasmaa turned the courtyard of Aleksanterinkatu 15 into one of the attractions of central Helsinki in 1991. His plan for the renovation of the KOP bank headquarters has unfortunately been shelved to await better times. For the Rovaniemi Art Museum, he conjured up a quietly persuasive building by making small alterations to an old postal bus station built after the war from bricks already

*Myyrmäki Church.
Juha Leiviskä, 1984;
textiles by Kristiina
Nyrhinen.*

used once for an earlier building. Five columns of Lapland stone draw passers-by into the magic circle of art.

In industrial architecture, a Constructivist use of steel gave the impetus to the work of Erkki Kairamo, Matti K. Mäkinen (1932–) and Kaarina Löfström (1941–). The Valio dairy and office buildings, designed by Mäkinen, proudly proclaim the importance of Finland's dairy industry; Löfström's terse Innopoli gives the 'high-tech village' of Otaniemi an eye-catching facade overlooking the busy Ring Road.

Simo (1944–) and Käpy Paavilainen (1947–) built a fortress wall for Olari Church (1981), defying the noisy roadside location to produce both an imposing facade and a sheltered courtyard in which old trees tell their tale of centuries of civilization. In their Kontula Church and parish centre (1988), the Paavilainens adopted a livelier idiom. The pluralistic interior contains several references to the Classicism of the '20s.

In the Church of Puolivälikangas in Oulu (1975), Juha Leiviskä developed his own set of themes for church architecture. Myyrmäki Church and parish centre in Vantaa (1984) lent the whole dreary housing area a new dignity and freshness. Leiviskä placed the long, closed back wall right next to the railway, saving the birches of the plot to create a park which gives space and air to the angular church building. Of the many

enthusiastic descriptions of the interior, that of William J.R. Curtis stands out: "[It] provides a sequence of spaces of such rhythmic beauty and musical intensity that one is justified in feeling that it is a work aspiring towards a sublime order. The suspended and overlapping planes of ceilings, walls and windows open to admit an indirect light that dissolves the boundaries of the senses and elevates the mind."

Georg Grotenfelt (1951–) has dedicated himself heart and soul to the Finnish landscape and the tradition of wood construction. His small saunas and summer cottages and the Land Settlement Association's Ararat Lodge in Juva (1986) offer delightful moments off the beaten track. They discreetly suggest that the regionalism that lives on in Europe's peripheral areas could with good reason be termed National Romanticism. In Grotenfelt's architecture, a reflective sense of locality lives as glowingly in the present as did Sonck's architecture in his day.

* * * *

All was quiet on the construction front in Finland in summer 1993. One third of all architects were unemployed: an unheard-of situation. Some did a lot of reading, some studied the environment with a camera; others sketched, dreaming of a new shape for the landscape.

Over five hundred entries were submitted in the architectural competition for the Museum of

Modern Art in Helsinki, more than ever before. There were many good plans. U.S. architect Steven Holl will build the museum, but many Finns have learned a great deal from the competition.

The last major competition before this was in 1989 for the design of the Finnish pavilion for the 1992 World's Fair in Seville. In the space of seven weeks, 157 entries were sent in under the theme "Finland – Creative by Nature". Everyone was happy to see victory go to 'Helvetinkolu' (Hell's Chasm), a design by five students. Juha Jääskeläinen, Juha Kaakko, Petri Rouhiainen, Matti Sanaksenaho and Jari Tirkkonen fulfilled the cherished dream of the Finnish architectural world, building a project of national importance as young unknowns.

The ascetic pavilion, consisting of a wooden keel, a metal machine and a dramatic interstice, remained in Seville. It held its own both in the international clamour of the exposition and in the silence that followed. Now it serves to uphold our belief that Finnish architecture truly still is creative by nature.

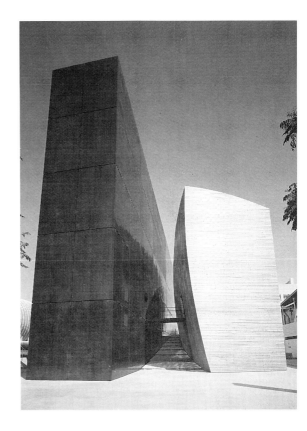

Finnish pavilion at the Seville World's Fair, summer 1992. Juha Jääskeläinen, Juha Kaakko, Petri Rouhiainen, Matti Sanaksenaho and Jari Tirkkonen.

SELECT BIBLIOGRAPHY

Ars Suomen taide 1–6. Otava 1987–1990.

Abacus 1–3. Vuosikirja.Yearbook. Museum of Finnish Architecture (MFA) 1979,1981,1983.

Acanthus 1990. Ed. Marja-Riitta Norri, Maija Kärkkäinen. MFA 1990.

Acanthus 1992. Ed. Riitta Nikula, Marja-Riitta Norri, Kristiina Paatero. MFA

Ålander, Kyösti, *Suomen teollisuuden arkkitehtuuria. Industriarkitektur i Finland. Industrial Architecture in Finland.* Association of Finnish Architects 1952.

An Architectural Present – 7 Approaches. Arkkitehtuurin nykyhetki – 7 näkökulmaa. Ed. Marja-Riitta Norri, Maija Kärkkäinen. MFA 1990.

Bertel Jung. Suurkaupungin hahmottaja. Helsinki City Planning Department 1988.

Betoni Suomessa 1860–1960. Suomen Betoniyhdistys 1991.

Blomstedt, Yrjö, Sucksdorff, Victor, *Karjalaisia rakennuksia ja koristemuotoja. Kuvasto.* Drawings collection. Helsinki 1900.

Carl Ludvig Engel 1778–1840. Exhibition in the Helsinki Cathedral crypt 1990.

Christ-Janer, Albert, *Eliel Saarinen.* The University of Chicago Press 1979.

Finland. Land of Natural Beauty. Ed. Pertti Kosonen. Oy Valitut Palat – Readers' Digest Ab. Helsinki 1989.

G. T. Chiewiz, lääninarkkitehti, länsarkitekt 1815–1862. Regional Central Museum of Turku 1987.

Connah, Roger, *Writing Architecture.* Rakennuskirja 1989.

Erik Bryggman 1891–1955. Arkkitehti, arkitekt, architect. Ed. Riitta Nikula. MFA 1991.

Frampton, Kenneth, *Modern Architecture, a critical History.* Thames & Hudson 1992.

Gardberg, C. J., *Stadsplan och byggnadsskick i Borgå intill år 1834.* Särtryck ur Folklivsstudier II. Helsingfors 1950.

af Hällström, Olof, *Sveaborg, Viapori, Suomenlinna. The Island Fortress off Helsinki.* Anders Nyborg A / S 1986.

Hämeen linna. Text by Elias Härö. National Board of Antiquities and Historical Monuments.

Hämeen linna. Text by Rainer Knapas. Association of Blind War Veterans 1973.

Hausen, Marika, Mikkola, Kirmo, Amberg, Anna-Lisa, Valto, Tytti, *Eliel Saarinen. Projects 1896–1923.* MFA and Otava 1990.

Heinonen, Raija-Liisa, *Funktionalismin läpimurto Suomessa.* MFA 1986.

Helamaa, Erkki, *40-luku. Korsujen ja jälleenrakentamisen vuosikymmen.* SRM, Alvar Aalto Museum 1983.

Helander, Vilhelm – Rista, Simo, *Suomalainen rakennustaide. Modern Architecture in Finland.* Kirjayhtymä 1989

Hiekkanen, Markus, *Rauma. Keskiajan kaupungit 2.* National Board of Antiquities and Historical Monuments 1983.

Hurme, Riitta, *Suomalainen lähiö Tapiolasta Pihlajamäkeen.* Societas Scientiarum Fennica 1991.

Ilonen, Arvi, *Helsinki, Espoo, Kauniainen, Vantaa. Architectural Guide.* Otava 1990.

J. S. Sirén. Arkkitehti, Architect 1889–1961. SRM. MFA 1989.

Järvelä-Hynynen, Raija, *Seurasaari. Kuvakirja ulkomuseosta. The Open-Air Museum in Pictures.* Museovirasto 1992.

Jokinen, Teppo, *Erkki Huttunen 1901–1956, arkkitehti.* Abacus ajankohta 3. MFA 1993.

Kaila, Panu, Pietarila, Pentti, Tomminen, Hannu, *Talo kautta aikojen. Julkisivujen historia.* Rakentajain Kustannus Oy 1987.

Keinänen, Timo & al., *Martti Välikangas 1893–1973, arkkitehti.* Abacus ajankohta 4. MFA 1993.

Kirkollisten rakennusten suojelutoimikunnan mietintö. Committee report 1986:5.

Kivinen, Paula, *Tampereen jugend. Arkkitehtuuri – taideteollisuus.* Otava 1982.

Klinge, Matti, *Brief History of Finland.* Otava 1992.

Klinge, Matti, *Senaatintorin sanoma.* Otava 1986.

Knapas, Marja Terttu, *Om kyrkobyggandet i Finland 1760–1809. Kyrkobyggnader 1760–1860.* Del 3. Övre Norrland. Sveriges kyrkor 217. 1993.

Knuttimring i Norden. Bidrag till dess äldre historia. Ed. Göran Rosander. Dalarnas Museum 1986.

Kolehmainen, Alfred, *Suomalainen talonpoikaistalo.* Otava 1979.

Kopisto, Sirkka, *Suomen Kansallismuseo.* National Board of Antiquities and Historical Monuments 1981.

Korvenmaa, Pekka, *Innovation versus tradition. The architect Lars Sonck. Works and projects 1900–1910.* SMYA 96. Helsinki 1991.

Laasonen, Pentti, *Suomen kirkon historia 2, vuodet 1593–1808.* WSOY 1991.

Lars Sonck, arkkitehti, architect 1870–1956. MFA 1981.

Lehtikanto, Mirjam, *Rakennettiin uusi Vaasa.* Vaasa 1981.

Lilius, Henrik, *Esplanadi, Esplanaden, The Esplanade.* Helsinki, Helsingborg. Anders Nyborg A / S 1984.

Lilius, Henrik, *Joensuu 1848–1890. Erään suomalaisen puukaupungin vaiheita.* Joensuu City Museums 1972.

Lilius, Henrik, *Suomalainen puukaupunki. Trästaden i Finland. The Finnish Wooden Town.* Anders Nyborg A / S 1985.

Lukkarinen, Ville, *Classicism and History. Anachronistic Architectural Thinking in Finland at the Turn of the Century. Jac. Ahrenberg and Gustaf Nyström.* SMYA 93. Helsinki 1989.

Lukkarinen, Ville, *Valtionarkiston satavuotias rakennus. Riksarkivets hundraåriga byggnad.* VAPK-Kustannus, Finnish State Archives 1990.

Meurman, Otto-I., *Asemakaavaoppi.* Otava 1947.

Mikkola, Kirmo, *Aalto.* Gummerus 1985.

Moorhouse, Jonathan, Carapetian, Michael, Ahtola-Moorhouse, Leena, *Helsingin jugendarkkitehtuuri 1895–1915.* Otava 1987.

Nikula, Riitta, *Armas Lindgren 1874–1929, arkkitehti, architect.* MFA 1988.

Nikula, Riitta, *Yhtenäinen kaupunkikuva 1900–1930.* Societas Scientiarum Fennica 1981.

Norri, Marja-Riitta, *Architecture in Miniature, Juhani Pallasmaa.* Raccolta Alvar Aalto alla biennale di Venezia, MFA 1991.

Norri, Marja-Riitta, *Pietilä.* MFA, Alvar Aalto Museum 1985.

Norri, Marja-Riitta, Kärkkäinen, Maija, *Aarno Ruusuvuori.* MFA 1992.

Pettersson, Lars, *Suomen kansanomainen rakennustaide.* Oma Maa 4. WSOY 1958.

Pöykkö, Kalevi, *Das Hauptgebäude der Kaiserlichen Alexander-Universität von Finnland.* SMYA 74. Helsinki 1972.

Profiles. Pioneering Women Architects from Finland. MFA 1983.

Putkonen, Lauri, *Kulttuurihistoriallisesti arvokkaat teollisuusympäristöt.* Ministry of the Environment 1988

Rakennushallitus Byggnadsstyrelsen 1811–1986. Toim. / Red. Juhani Pallasmaa. National Board of Building, MFA 1986.

Ringbom, Sixten, *Stone, Style and Truth. The vogue for natural stone in Nordic architecture 1880–1910.* SMYA 91. Helsinki 1987.

Saarikangas, Kirsi, *Model Houses for Model Families. Gender, Ideology and the Modern Dwelling.* The Type-Planned Houses of the 1940s in Finland. Finnish Historical Society 1993.

Schildt, Göran, *Alvar Aalto. The Decisive Years.* Otava 1986.

Schildt, Göran, *Alvar Aalto. The Early Years.* Rizzoli 1984.

Schildt, Göran, *Alvar Aalto. The Mature Years.* Rizzoli 1991.

Sinisalo, Antero, *500-vuotias Olavinlinna.* Helsinki 1976.

Suomalainen puukirkko. Finnish Wooden Church. Text by Lars Pettersson, Marja Terttu Knapas, Riitta Nikula, Kristiina Paatero. MFA. Otava 1992.

Suomalaista kaupunkiarkkitehtuuria. Finnish Town Planning and Architecture. Ed. Jussi Kautto, Ilkka Holmila, Jukka Turtiainen. MFA, Ministry of the Environment 1990.

Suomen Historia 1–2. Weilin & Göös 1984–1985.

Suomen Kaupunkilaitoksen historia 1–3. Association of Finnish Cities 1981–1984.

Suomen rakennustaiteen museon arkisto, piirustuskokoelma. Archives of the Museum of Finnish Architecture, Drawings Collection. 1989.

Suomi rakentaa, Finland bygger, Finland Builds 1–8. Exhibition catalogues 1953–1992.

Suominen-Kokkonen, Renja, *The Fringe of a Profession. Women as Architects in Finland from the 1890s to the 1950s.* SMYA 98. Helsinki 1992.

Talve, Ilmar, *Suomen kansankulttuuri.* Finnish Literature Society 1979.

Tuomi, Timo, *Tapiola. Puutarhakaupungin vaiheita. Arkkitehtuuriopas.* Espoo City Museum 1992.

Valanto, Sirkka, *Rautateiden arkkitehtuuri. Järnvägarnas arkitektur.* MFA, Alvar Aalto Museum 1984.

Valonen, Niilo, *Seurasaari, ulkomuseo / open-air museum.* Otava 1973.

Valonen, Niilo, *Zur Geschichte der Finnischen Wohnstuben.* Helsinki 1963.

Vanha Rauma. Text by Anna Nurmi-Nielsen, Jukka Koivula et al. Urban community development campaign. Publication No. 2 / 1982.

Viipurin linna. Text by Sampo Ahto. Association of Blind War Veterans. Otava 1968.

Viljo Revell. Ed. Kyösti Ålander. Otava 1968.

Viljo, Eeva Maija, *Theodor Höijer. En arkitekt under den moderna storstadsarkitekturens genombrottstid i Finland från 1870 till sekelskiftet.* SMYA 88. Helsinki 1985.

Wäre, Ritva, *Rakennettu suomalaisuus. Nationalismi viime vuosisadan vaihteen arkkitehtuurissa ja sitä koskevissa kirjoituksissa.* SMYA 95. Helsinki 1991.

Wickberg, Nils Erik, *Senaatintori. Senatstorget. The Senate Square. Der Senatsplatz.* Helsinki, Helsingborg. Anders Nyborg A / S 1981.

Yliopiston Helsinki. Ed. Eea Pekkala-Koskela. University of Helsinki, Sanomaprint 1989.

Zetterberg, Seppo, *Finland after 1917.* Otava 1991.

PLACE INDEX

PHOTOGRAPHS

Photoarchives of Otava Publishing Company

AND

Museum of Finnish Architecture (MFA): p. 24, 54 left, 93, 94,
    98, 100, 111, 112, 113, 114, 115, 116.
MFA / Apollo: p. 103.
MFA / Arne von Boehm: p. 146.
MFA / Fotark: p. 151 middle.
MFA / Foto Roos: p. 92, 118, 126, 127, 129.
MFA / Kari Hakli: p. 16, 40, 43, 51, 53, 61, 79, 80, 82, 86, 90, 91,
    97, 121, 122, 123.
MFA / Heikki Havas: p. 104, 131, 135, 140, 144.
MFA / I. K. Inha: p. 8.
MFA / Risto Kamunen: p. 77.
MFA / Arto Kiviniemi: p. 141.
MFA / Jarmo Knuuttila: p. 154.
MFA / Pekka Laurila: p. 75, 120, 134.
MFA / Olli Lehtovuori: p. 137.
MFA / Matilainen: p. 139.
MFA / Raili Pietilä: p. 150.
MFA / Otso Pietinen: p. 101, 102, 145.
MFA / Lauri Putkonen: p. 83.
MFA / Istvan Rácz: p. 20, 44 right.
MFA / Pekka Rajala: p. 139.
MFA / Juhani Riekkola: p. 150.
MFA / Simo Rista: p. 6, 56 below, 64, 69, 119, 134, 136, 146.
MFA / Loja Saarinen: p. 99.
MFA / Asko Salokorpi: p. 84.
MFA / Thomas Rory Spence: p. 108.
MFA / Eric Sundström: p. 106.
MFA / V. A. Wahlström: p. 130.
MFA / Gustaf Welin: p. 132.
MFA / P. O. Welin: p. 29.
MFA / N. E. Wickberg: p. 30, 52 right, 81, 124.

Asuntosäätiö / Housing Foundation: p. 147.
Georg Grotenfelt: p. 153.
Reto Halme: p. 155.
Helsinki City Museum: p. 78, 87, 89, 102 left.
National Board of Antiquities and Historical Monuments:
    p. 27, 35, 59, 71 right.
Riitta Nikula: p. 23 right, 42, 71, 102 right, 149, 151 above.
Eero Pettersson: p. 45 right.
Harald Raebiger: p. 60.
Mikko Suurpää: p. 74.
Rauno Träskelin: p. 63 left, 65, 148, 151 below.
Al Weber: p. 152.